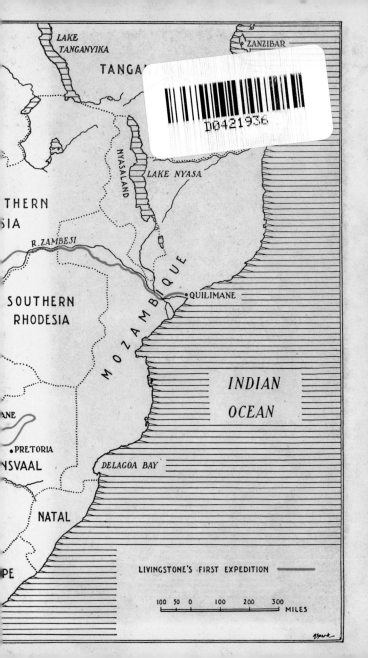

LAKE
TANGANYIKA

ZANZIBAR

TANGA

D0421936

LAKE NYASA

THERN
SIA

NYASALAND

R. ZAMBESI

SOUTHERN
RHODESIA

MOZAMBIQUE

QUILIMANE

ANE

PRETORIA

NSVAAL

NATAL

PE

INDIAN

OCEAN

DELAGOA BAY

LIVINGSTONE'S FIRST EXPEDITION

100 50 0   100   200   300
                                    MILES

LIVINGSTONE

AND

AFRICA

is one of the volumes
in the
TEACH YOURSELF HISTORY
LIBRARY

Edited by A. L. ROWSE

Teach Yourself History

VOLUMES READY OR IN PREPARATION

The Use of History, by A. L. Rowse
Pericles and Athens, by A. R. Burn
Alexander the Great and the Hellenistic Empire, by A. R. Burn
Agricola and Roman Britain, by A. R. Burn
Constantine and the Conversion of Europe, by A. H. M. Jones
Charlemagne and Western Europe, by H. St. L. B. Moss
Wycliffe and the Beginnings of English Nonconformity,
  by K. B. McFarlane
Henry V and the Invasion of France, by E. F. Jacob
Joan of Arc and the Recovery of France, by Alice Buchan
Lorenzo dei Medici and Renaissance Italy, by C. M. Ady
Erasmus and the Northern Renaissance, by Margaret Mann Phillips
Cranmer and the English Reformation, by F. E. Hutchinson
Whitgift and the English Church, by V. J. K. Brook
Raleigh and the British Empire, by D. B. Quinn
Richelieu and the French Monarchy, by C. V. Wedgwood
Cromwell and the Puritan Revolution, by Mary Coate
Milton and the English Mind, by F. E. Hutchinson
Louis XIV and the Greatness of France, by Maurice Ashley
Peter the Great and the Emergence of Russia, by B. H. Sumner
Chatham and the British Empire, by Sir Charles Grant Robertson
Cook and the Opening of the Pacific, by James A. Williamson
Catherine the Great and the Expansion of Russia,
  by Gladys Scott Thomson
Warren Hastings and British India, by Penderel Moon
Washington and the American Revolution, by Esmond Wright
Robespierre and the French Revolution, by J. M. Thompson
Napoleon and the Awakening of Europe, by F. M. H. Markham
Bolivar and the Independence of Spanish America, by J. B. Trend
Jefferson and American Democracy, by Max Beloff
Pushkin and Russian Literature, by Janko Lavrin
Abraham Lincoln and the United States, by K. C. Wheare
Napoleon III and the Second Empire, by J. P. T. Bury
Livingstone and Africa, by Jack Simmons
Gladstone and Liberalism, by J. L. Hammond and M. R. D. Foot
Clemenceau and the Third Republic, by J. Hampden Jackson
Woodrow Wilson and American Liberalism, by E. M. Hugh-Jones
Lenin and the Russian Revolution, by Christopher Hill
Botha, Smuts and South Africa, by Basil Williams
Gandhi and Modern India, by Guy Wint

DAVID LIVINGSTONE
From a photograph taken by Thomas Annan
at Glasgow, 1864

LIVINGSTONE

AND

AFRICA

by
JACK SIMMONS

7078

ENGLISH UNIVERSITIES PRESS LTD
102, NEWGATE STREET,
LONDON E.C.I.

FIRST PRINTED 1955

PRINTED AND BOUND IN ENGLAND
FOR THE ENGLISH UNIVERSITIES PRESS, LTD.,
BY HAZELL WATSON AND VINEY LTD., AYLESBURY

A General Introduction
to the Series

THIS series has been undertaken in the conviction
that there can be no subject of study more important
than history. Great as have been the conquests of natural
science in our time—such that many think of ours as a
scientific age *par excellence*—it is even more urgent and
necessary that advances should be made in the social
sciences if we are to gain control of the forces of nature
loosed upon us. The bed out of which all the social
sciences spring is history; there they find, in greater or
lesser degree, subject-matter and material, verification or
contradiction.

There is no end to what we can learn from history, if
only we will, for it is coterminous with life. Its special
field is the life of man in society, and at every point we
can learn vicariously from the experience of others before
us in history.

To take one point only—the understanding of politics:
how can we hope to understand the world of affairs
around us if we do not know how it came to be what it
is? How to understand Germany, or Soviet Russia, or the
United States—or ourselves—without knowing something
of their history?

There is no subject that is more useful or, indeed,
indispensable.

Some evidence of the growing awareness of this may be
seen in the immense increase in the interest of the reading public in history and the much larger place the subject has come to take in education in our time.

This series has been planned to meet the needs and

demands of a very wide public and of education—they are, indeed, the same. I am convinced that the most congenial, as well as the most concrete and practical, approach to history is the biographical, through the lives of the great men whose actions have been so much part of history, and whose careers in turn have been so moulded and formed by events.

The key-idea of this series, and what distinguishes it from any other that has appeared, is the intention by way of a biography of a great man to open up a significant historical theme; for example, Cromwell and the Puritan Revolution, or Lenin and the Russian Revolution.

My hope is, in the end, as the series fills out and completes itself, by a sufficient number of biographies to cover whole periods and subjects in that way. To give you the history of the United States, for example, or the British Empire or France, *via* a number of biographies of their leading historical figures.

That should be something new, as well as convenient and practical, in education.

I need hardly say that I am a strong believer in people with good academic standards writing once more for the general reading public, and of the public being given the best that the universities can provide. From this point of view this series is intended to bring the university into the homes of the people.

A. L. ROWSE

ALL SOULS COLLEGE
OXFORD

Contents

Introductory Note

THE great historical theme with which this book is concerned is the opening-up of Africa in the nineteenth century. Livingstone may or may not have been the greatest of all African explorers—though, taking everything into account, I think few people who are qualified to judge would deny him that title. What is even more important is the influence that he has exercised over the policy pursued by Europeans towards Africa in the course of the past hundred years. He has affected the thinking of all of us, about Africa and about Africans. This book tries to show what Africa was like when Livingstone's work began, the ideas that were current in Europe concerning the continent and its people; and then the effect that Livingstone's own work and teaching had in changing those ideas, in leading on towards the very different attitude that has come to be accepted since his death.

I should like to add a word about the spelling of African proper names in this book. In general I have followed two rules : to use the form that is most simply grasped by English readers, and to keep as close as possible to the spelling that Livingstone himself used. I am aware that this sometimes involves anomalies, and that it will not please expert philologists. But I hope even they will admit that, for the ordinary reader, "uMzilikazi" is a rather forbidding proposition, not readily equated with the familiar form "Mosilikatse" used by Livingstone.

I have thought it best to omit accents throughout. It should be understood that the final "e" in East African place-names is almost always pronounced separately, as if it bore a French acute accent : "Shire" is therefore a two-syllabled word, its pronunciation as near as possible to "Sheeray".

Chapter One

Early Years
(1813–1841)

DAVID LIVINGSTONE was born at Blantyre, near
Glasgow, on 19 March 1813. His parents were
Neil Livingstone, who was of Highland descent, and
Agnes Hunter, a Lowlander. Since the blending of Highland and Lowland strains made an important element in
the explorer's character, something must be said of the
families from which his parents sprang.

His paternal grandfather, Neil Livingstone,[1] was a
small farmer in the island of Ulva. His story is characteristic of eighteenth-century Scotland. He was one of the
thousands who were driven to leave the Highlands by the
great expansion of sheep-farming there : the sheep were
pastured in the valleys in winter, and the smallholders
evicted to make room for them. The greater part of the
emigrants found their way to North America and Australia, but some moved instead into the towns of the
Scottish Lowlands, whose industry was then developing
rapidly. Among them was Neil Livingstone, who left
Ulva in 1792 with the declared purpose of securing
employment in a cotton-mill. He found the work he
wanted with the firm of Monteith & Co. at Blantyre, who
treated him well and gave him a position of trust. In due
course his five sons entered the business, too—not as

[1] The Livingstones habitually spelt their name without the
final "e". The explorer followed his family's practice until 1855,
when he abandoned "Livingston". In this book the familiar form
of the name will be used throughout.

factory hands but as clerks, for they had had a sound education. One of them, Charles, became head clerk in Monteith's Glasgow office; but he had the bad luck to be seized by the press-gang, and died young on active service in the navy in the Mediterranean. All the rest, except one, left Blantyre to fight in the Napoleonic wars : it is said that the three brothers were all present at Waterloo.

The one who stayed behind was Neil, the explorer's father; and though he was of a less adventurous spirit than his brothers, he too presently left Monteith's. He was apprenticed for a time to a tailor named David Hunter; but he soon abandoned tailoring, to become an itinerant tea-dealer. He sold his wares with a scrupulous honesty, and always remained poor. But he liked the work because it gave scope to the passionate interest of his life—religion, the dissemination of the Gospel. Together with his teas he distributed religious tracts. He took a delight in theological conversation and argument, in which he maintained a stubborn independence that led him in the end to secede from the Church of Scotland and become a deacon in a separate church established at Hamilton, three miles from Blantyre. He was a rigid teetotaller—something rare and ridiculous then. He had the fiery temper of his people, and he was strict in enforcing his own standards of conduct on his children. But they loved him deeply, none the less. As David afterwards wrote of him : "By his kindliness of manner and winning ways he made the heartstrings of his children twine around him as firmly as if he had possessed, and could have bestowed upon them, every worldly advantage. . . . I revere his memory."

Neil Livingstone married in 1810. His wife was the daughter of David Hunter, the tailor to whom he had been apprenticed. Hunter, too, like Neil's father, was a countryman who had migrated into the suburbs of Glasgow. He came from Shotts in the Lanarkshire uplands, of a farming family with a marked Covenanting tradition. But he was of a gentler nature than the tough Livingstones : it is recorded of him that he had to give up farming because he had lent more than he could afford to his poorer neighbours. He took to tailoring instead, and was engaged by Monteith & Co. to make clothes for the orphan children they employed at Blantyre.

Agnes Hunter inherited from her father his quiet, steady religious convictions and his gentle and kindly disposition. She did something, it is plain, to soften the angularity of her severe, rather formidable husband. She was a most careful housewife, and an excellent mother to her children, who were devoted to her. Like Scott's mother, she transmitted to her great son a store of reminiscences and traditional tales; as late as 1864, when she was in her eighty-second year, we find him noting down one of them in his journal, straight from her lips. She died in 1865.

On the tombstone over the grave of Neil and Agnes Livingstone in Hamilton cemetery there is an inscription recording their children's "thankfulness to God . . . for poor and pious parents". The simple phrase was written by the explorer himself. He always took an intense pride in the class from which he sprang—"my own order," he called it, "the honest poor". He owed a great deal to his parents, and their characters can be seen in him, magnified to an heroic scale. From his father's side came his tenacity, his independence, his obstinacy, the harsh dourness that sometimes alienated his associates, and two specifically Celtic traits : the mercurial rising and falling of his spirits and the imagination, the sense of poetry, that flashes momentarily across his mind. His mother contributed much to the gentler side of his nature, above all to the tenderness and patience that never failed him with Africans. From both his parents he inherited a strong common sense and the serene, unshakeable religion that dominated and inspired all his work.

David was their second surviving child. He had an elder brother (John), a younger brother (Charles), and two sisters (Janet and Agnes). There is nothing exceptional to record of his childhood. He was put to school early, in the good Scottish manner; but he made no great mark there, though he was always studious. "He was aye lyin' on his belly readin' a book"—that was the verdict passed on him by a farmer who tried employing him to mind his cattle, and soon gave up the experiment. Blantyre, indeed, found David Livingstone somewhat unaccountable: "a sulky, quiet, feckless sort o' boy", nothing more.

At the age of ten he went to work in the cotton-mill. He started as a "piecer", whose job was to look after the spinning jenny and tie up broken threads. The work was not arduous in itself, but the hours were extremely long— from six in the morning till eight at night, with two intervals for meals. On top of that for two more hours there was a night school to be attended, for Messrs. Monteith were good employers who were careful to observe the Factory Act of 1802, which provided for the education of children working in cotton-mills.

He remained in the mill from 1823 to 1836. But he made up his mind very early that he was not going to stay there for the rest of his life. Education clearly provided the best means by which he could hope to escape from the mill, and he began to pursue learning tenaciously. It was the boy's habit to fix a Latin grammar on his spinning jenny, which he could study—in snatches, perhaps of a minute at a time—as he passed and re-passed at his work. The mill girls, we are told, amused themselves by throwing bobbins at the book to knock it down. But it made no difference to him. He went on at his Latin, philosophically, just the same; and in after years he attributed much of his power of abstracting his mind from the noises around him when he was in Africa to the severe training in mental concentration that he had gone through in the mill at Blantyre.

He has himself preserved for us one other revealing glimpse of these early years, in a casual sentence of a letter written to his brother-in-law in 1858: "When I was a piecer, the fellows used to try to turn me off from the

4

path I had chosen, and always began with 'I think you ought, etc.', till I snapped them up with a mild 'You *think*! I can *think* and *act* for myself; don't need anybody to think for me, I assure you.'" And then he adds the characteristic comment : "This must, according to my experience, be the way all through. I never followed another's views in preference to my own judgment, i.e. did a thing out of deference to another when I myself thought it wrong, but I had reason to repent of it." Livingstone's character and ideas always remained singularly consistent. He owed much of both to his early experience in the cotton-mill. Above all, it was there that his ruthless, steel-like determination was forged.

He certainly needed it all. When he was eighteen he was promoted to be a "spinner". It meant greater responsibility and better pay; but the work was physically much more exacting—he described it long afterwards as "excessively severe on a slim, loose-jointed lad", and he was never given to self-pity. Still, however, his toil at his books continued, at the end of the long day's spinning.

By now he was reading for a quite definite end. His father's religious interests had extended to Christian missions abroad, and it was through him that David first became aware of their work. He soon made up his mind to become a missionary himself. But not a preacher of the Gospel alone. His mind was fired by what he read of the medical missionaries—a new species then, just beginning to go forth. He had always had a streak of the scientist in him : Culpeper's *Herbal* was one of the books in which he took the greatest pleasure; he and his brothers had been accustomed to go on long botanising expeditions, whenever they had the time, far out into the surrounding countryside. This taste steadily developed in him, and as he grew up the course in front of him became clear : he must qualify as a doctor and then go out in the service of a missionary society—to China if possible, for that was his chosen field.

When he was twenty-three he had saved enough money

to enable him to begin his studies at Glasgow. Accordingly, in the autumn of 1836 he entered Anderson's College, moving into lodgings in the town, which cost him half-a-crown a week. Directly the session was over, in the spring of 1837, he moved back to Blantyre, working in the mill through the summer in order to earn enough to keep himself for the following session : then back to Glasgow for a second spell in the winter of 1837–1838. Though medicine was his prime study, it was not his only one. Following the Scottish tradition, he attended a wide range of lectures, in theology, chemistry, Greek. Among his fellow-students were Lyon Playfair and the future Lord Kelvin; and James Young, the assistant to the professor of chemistry, became his friend. Twenty years afterwards Young grew rich through his discovery of a means of extracting paraffin from coal, and he contributed liberally to the assistance of Livingstone on his last journey.

As his second session at Glasgow drew to a close he wrote to the London Missionary Society, offering it his services. He chose that society for a special reason : because it was unsectarian, sending "neither episcopacy, nor presbyterianism, nor independency, but the gospel of Christ to the heathen". Yet though he approved of the Society's methods, it was only after a struggle that he brought himself to apply to it at all. Again the reason is typical of him : "It was not quite agreeable to one accustomed to work his own way to become in a measure dependent on others. And I would not have been much put about, though my offer had been rejected."

It was favourably received, however, and in August 1838 he went up to London for an interview with the Directors of the Society. After two examinations, he was sent, as a probationer, to study under the Rev. Richard Cecil at Ongar in Essex. He lived in lodgings with a fellow-student, going daily to Mr. Cecil to be instructed in theology and the classics. It was a part of their training to compose sermons. When these had been corrected by the tutor, they were memorised by the students, who were sent to deliver them in the chapels of neighbouring villages. Livingstone went out to preach at Stanford Rivers one evening, but when he got into the pulpit his sermon vanished from his mind. Overcome with confusion, he blurted out, "Friends, I have forgotten all I had to say", and rushed from the chapel.

Such episodes disquieted his tutor. When the time came for a report on the probationer it was, naturally, not wholly favourable. He might easily have been dismissed on the spot as unsuited for the Society's work if one of the Directors had not spoken up in his favour and secured him a second chance. He was sent back to Ongar, and this time he gained a better opinion from his tutor and was fully accepted by the Society. In January 1840 he moved to London to resume his medical studies there. At Glasgow his work had been almost entirely theoretical; what he needed now was some practical experience, and this he gained at the Charing Cross Hospital and at Moorfields. He worked under Dr. Risdon Bennett (who afterwards had a distinguished career and became President of the Royal College of Physicians). At the same time, to enlarge his knowledge of anatomy, he frequented the Hunterian Museum. He soon became friendly with its curator, Richard Owen. Their friendship was life-long. Owen grew into one of the most famous scientists of his day, though he is chiefly remembered now as a leading opponent of the theory of natural selection, which he attacked with a crazy and disagreeable ferocity. This friendship shows him in a better light : he paid Livingstone a fine tribute, after his death, in the *Quarterly Review* in 1875.

Livingstone made several such friendships in his student days, and he went on adding to their number throughout his life. He constantly corresponded with his friends, always thought and spoke of them with warmth, and helped them loyally when it was in his power. At the same time it may be doubted if he was ever really intimate with any of them, for his friendships tended rather to be affectionate alliances in a common cause. At heart he was solitary, withdrawn—even now, before his long isolation in Africa. And besides, like all the great, he had much of the egoist in him.

He was already a personality : provincial and awkward on the surface, but clearly powerful underneath. "He has sense and quiet vigour," Mr. Cecil reported; "his temper is good and his character substantial." A more revealing hint comes from the fellow-student who knew him best: "There was truly an indescribable charm about him, which, with all his rather ungainly ways, and by no means winning face, attracted almost every one. . . . He won those who came near him by a kind of spell." Here again is the Highlander in him : Englishmen and Africans alike were susceptible to that wonderful Celtic charm.

His original desire, as we have seen, had been to work as a missionary in China. But the "Opium War" broke out while he was a student at Ongar, and that closed the country to missions for the time being. Instead, the Directors proposed to send him to the West Indies. He at once protested with energy: "Settling in the West Indies", he firmly told them, "has always appeared to me so much like the ministry at home that my thoughts have not at all been attracted in that direction, but always to other parts of the world." He was already thinking of Africa when by chance he met Robert Moffat, one of the best known missionaries of the age, home on leave from Bechuanaland. They had several talks together, and then one day he asked if Moffat thought he "would do for Africa". Moffat's reply is memorable, for it provided the text for the whole of the rest of Livingstone's life : "I said I believed he would, if he would not go to an old station, but would advance to unoccupied ground, specifying the vast plain to the north, where I had sometimes seen, in the morning sun, the smoke of a thousand villages, where no missionary had ever been." Here, beyond a doubt, was the work the young man wanted: one can almost hear the "call" in Moffat's words. His career was decided. He would go to Africa.

His training now drew to an end; but it was interrupted by a dangerous illness, affecting his lungs. It was decided that the best chance of saving his life lay in sending him home to Scotland by sea, in the hope that the voyage and his native air would cure him. They did. He returned to London in sound health, to prepare for his departure. In November 1840 he made a final, fleeting visit to Glasgow to be examined for his Licentiate of the Faculty of Physicians and Surgeons of the university. He secured the degree; but he nearly missed it through an injudicious obstinacy in arguing with his examiners about the use of the stethoscope. He spent that night at home, and the following morning his father walked down with him into Glasgow to see him off by the Liverpool steamer. They never met again.

Directly he arrived in London he was ordained as a missionary in the Albion Chapel, and little more than a fortnight later, on 8 December 1840, he sailed in the *George* for South Africa.

Chapter Two

Africa in 1840

THE Africa that Livingstone was bound for was an almost unknown continent. In European tradition it was a vast and totally mysterious land, famed chiefly for the strange creatures and phenomena of nature that it produced—pygmies and giants and cannibals and subterranean rivers. When Sir Thomas Browne, in the seventeenth century, wished to express the astonishment he felt at the construction of the human frame, he wrote : "We carry with us the wonders that we seek without us. There is all Africa and her prodigies in us." That remained the attitude of most Europeans towards Africa until the later part of the nineteenth century.

It is true that a great deal had been done by European explorers to enlarge the knowledge of Africa and of its geography, physical and human. Its northern and northeastern shores had been known to the Ancients. In the course of the fifteenth century the Portuguese nosed their way down the whole of the western coast, rounded the Cape of Good Hope, and then sailed up the east coast as far as Cape Guardafui and so across to India. During the sixteenth century they learnt much more about the African coast, and gradually their knowledge found its way on to the charts and maps produced in Europe. But the attention of the Portuguese was directed almost entirely to the coast. They established trading-stations there for two purposes. Some, like Mozambique in the southeast, were intended primarily as bases for the victualling and repair of their ships on the long voyage to India and the Far East; others, like Elmina on the Gold Coast, were markets, magnets to draw goods from the interior, which could then be conveyed easily back to Lisbon. On the Gold Coast, indeed, the Portuguese do not seem to have made the smallest attempt to penetrate inland; they merely waited for trade to be brought to them by the Africans. Farther south, in their colony of Angola, they were a little more enterprising. But, as we shall see, even in 1854 Livingstone found their dominion here very slight, and it had never been much stronger. In the south-east, the Portuguese made some effort to discover what lay up the Zambesi valley, and their highest permanent station on the river, Tete, was some 300 miles from its mouth. But they could not claim any thorough knowledge of the interior, and they knew nothing whatever of the country farther north—what we now call Tanganyika and Kenya —apart from a few isolated towns and villages on the coast.

If the Portuguese knew little of Africa, no other people, before the nineteenth century, could boast of knowing more. When the Dutch East India Company established its post at Capetown in 1652, it deliberately tried to prevent the settlers from visiting the hinterland; naturally from its own point of view, since Capetown was designed solely as a calling-station for Dutch ships *en route* for the East, and a small, concentrated settlement was therefore required, not a widely-dispersed agricultural community. The Boer farmers were not amenable to the Company's control, and they disobeyed its instructions, "trekking" off to the north-east and east to establish their great, lonely farms beyond its effective jurisdiction. Settling in this way, with the disapproval of authority, it was not to be expected that the Boers should publish accounts of the country they lived in; and of their few visitors, very few indeed thought it worth while to describe their experiences.

The other European powers interested in Africa were France and England. Both held a number of small trading-posts on the west coast, between Cape Verde and the

Niger. But these posts were for trade and nothing else; and, like the Portuguese, the French and the English were content to absorb whatever trade was brought down to them by Africans, without making any effort to penetrate the interior. As for East Africa, by the beginning of the eighteenth century the Arabs had driven the Portuguese out of the towns they had held north of the River Rovuma. No European power had any pretensions there whatever.

Until the close of the eighteenth century, then, the continent of Africa was known to Europe as little more than an outline. It was in the 1780s that a new interest in the geographical problems of its interior began to emerge. This interest had a threefold origin. It was in part scientific, resulting from the great stimulus given by the Pacific discoveries of Bougainville and Cook to exploration all over the world. Again, it was commercial —the desire of new mechanised industries for products that Africa could, or might, furnish. And lastly it was humanitarian : for many of those who supported the exploration of Africa did so in the belief that if its interior could be thoroughly investigated, the source of supply of slaves would be found and the slave trade could then be killed at its roots.

The first great effort was made in West Africa : an assault on the problem of the River Niger. When it began, very little more was known about the river than Herodotus had gathered and recorded over two thousand years earlier. In less than half a century (1788-1830) the problem was solved, the Niger traced from source to mouth. Moreover, the swarm of explorers who had concentrated their efforts on the problem had done much towards the solution of others. They gained first-hand knowledge of the great Arab caravan-routes that ran north and south across the Sahara; they visited and described the Muslim states of what we now call Northern Nigeria; they even made a small start on the other great river-problem of western Africa, one that Livingstone

himself was concerned with in the closing years of his life
—the problem of the Congo.

It may perhaps be wondered why the questions presented by these rivers should have been so hard to solve.
Why not sail up or down them as the European travellers
sailed up and down the Ganges or the Mississippi? The
answer is to be found in the physical nature of the
African rivers themselves. The four great ones—Nile,
Niger, Congo, Zambesi—are all difficult to navigate,
from their rapids and from the intricate and swampy
deltas that impede their outlet to the sea. None of them,
except the lower Nile, has been historically a thriving
highway of trade. In many ways it is true to say that the
rivers were a hindrance rather than a help to the development of Africa before the nineteenth century. They did
not bring wealth and a flourishing trade, like most of the
other great rivers of the world: to many of the people who
lived near their banks they brought nothing but in-
security, a route by which hostile neighbours could move
conveniently to attack them.

The solution of the problem of the Niger coincided in
time with the greatest onslaught on the Atlantic slave trade:
the two things were, as we have seen, connected together.
In 1807 the trade was made illegal to British subjects;
within the next thirty years all the major European
governments agreed to prohibit their own people from
engaging in it; a squadron of the British Navy was
stationed on the west coast of Africa to seize the slave-
ships and release their cargoes. Furthermore, in 1833 the
British government passed the Act of Emancipation,
which brought the status of slavery itself to an end
throughout the British Empire. Altogether it was a
determined and vigorous attempt to destroy the slave
trade, and ultimately slavery, throughout the western
hemisphere.

But it fell short of complete success. Some powers,
notably France and the United States, were unwilling to
enforce an absolute prohibition of slave trading on their

subjects; and until the American Civil War slavery itself continued to be recognised in some of the United States. Moreover, for all the treaties and the naval squadrons, a surreptitious slave trade continued across the Atlantic. It found some obscure bases in West Africa, mainly in Portuguese and French territory. But as slaves became harder and harder to maintain, an altogether fresh source began to be exploited—the south-east coast. When Livingstone first went out to Africa, this new trade was only just beginning. Its destruction, and that of the great eastward slave trade that was bound up with it, became the dominant objective of the later part of his life.

The ordinary Englishman, when he thought of Africa in 1840, still thought of it in the vaguest terms. The maps, if he looked at them, would now help him a little more; great tracts of the north-west, which had previously been left blank or filled in with conjectures, were now mapped, if not quite accurately at any rate with a general approximation to the truth. But the rest of Africa was as little known as ever. In some ways the work of the Niger explorers had made the continent even more mysterious. For in describing the people and the societies they found, it was their instinctive tendency to emphasise the strangeness, the differences between African ideas and European. "Mumbo Jumbo" provides a good example. The religious ceremonies associated with Mumbo Jumbo were first described in English in 1738. They became very much more widely known through Mungo Park's description, first printed in 1799. But it was in the 1840s that the phrase came to be used in the sense it ordinarily bears today, applied to an idol that is treated with absurd respect. It was just such oddities as Mumbo Jumbo that stuck in Englishmen's minds, helping to complete their vague image of Africa—the obscurest, most impenetrable of the five continents, filled with wild people following strange customs and engaged in constant warfare, with the sole object of selling their neighbours into slavery.

It was, in some ways, a grotesque caricature. Yet it is

easy to see how the impression was formed. For while the travellers had described the great obstacles they met with and the quarrels and wars that they witnessed, none of them had set himself to study Africans as human beings. There are such studies—little portraits and vignettes that adorn their narratives, such as Park's account of the woman who looked after him with such tender care near Sego. Occasionally, too, the travellers attempted to describe a political situation or the structure of a government. But when they did so, they could rarely rise above the temptation to guy it, laying stress upon its apparent absurdities, its difference from the kind of government they knew at home. And in any case, all such portraits and descriptions are purely incidental to the travellers' main theme, an account of their own journeys. Delightful, and sometimes exciting, though their narratives are, they cannot be said to give their readers a very clear—still less a quite true—account of Africans and their societies. The first African traveller who consciously attempted this task, and with success, was not an Englishman but a German : Heinrich Barth, who moved slowly about in the western Sudan, describing and analysing everything he saw, in 1849–1855.

One important group of travellers might fairly have been expected to describe Africans and their ways, and to interpret them to their countrymen at home : the Christian missionaries. For exploration was not their first business. If they were travellers, it was always in a cause; and that cause was the spiritual welfare of the Africans themselves. It is no reflection at all on the sincerity of their intentions, or on the admirable and thankless work that many of them did on behalf of their people, if one says that the early nineteenth-century missionaries were too deeply imbued with the sense of their religious task to be able to give a clear and coherent account of the Africans among whom they lived. Most of them, too, had been bred in a narrow Evangelical tradition. How could they possibly stand outside it, to look with understanding, and without passion or disapproval, at these pagan, dark-skinned people? If the Englishman's impression of Africans was chiefly of their oddities and savagery, the utter difference between their standards and practices and his, that impression was fortified by the writings of the missionaries until it became fixed, almost immovably, in his mind. Moreover, the missionaries' assumption of the truth of Christianity, and the falsehood and wickedness of all pagan beliefs and practices, had the effect of making Englishmen complacently certain of their own superiority to Africans, in matters of the spirit as well as in technical and political accomplishment. This was not the missionaries' intention; but their naïve assumptions were made so plain, they were so sure they were right, and their public was so large and devoted, that this consequence inevitably followed.

By way of illustration, let us consider a few passages from the writings of Robert Moffat. Moffat gave the whole of his long working life to Africa. He went out there in the autumn of 1817, before he was twenty-one, and with the exception of a single visit home he remained there until 1870. He worked almost all that time in Bechuanaland, saving a series of expeditions he made to visit Mosilikatse, the great chief of the Matebele, to the north-east. From his private papers and from other accounts we have of him, he emerges as an entirely admirable man, kindly, self-denying, sensible, not without humour, above all incredibly patient. Yet what are his considered judgments on the people to whom he devoted himself? Of the Bushmen he remarked that "we can scarcely conceive of human beings descending lower in the scale of ignorance and vice; while yet there can be no question that they are children of one common parent with ourselves". As for the Matebele, the powerful, aggressive warriors, well disciplined under their formidable ruler, he came to regard them almost with despair.

During his second visit to them, on Sunday 19 July 1835, he wrote : "There has been much dancing and singing today. . . . It is a terrible barrier, not to know the language of a people who are dancing on to everlasting destruction." The next visit, in 1854, brought this comment : "I never lie down without feeling a degree of melancholy steal over me. One gets or must get accustomed to the naked *hurdies* of both men and women, but to view their ignorance, their degradation, their wallowing in wickedness, their veto on Christian instruction in connection with their eternal states, makes one wish they had not been. . . . They are become wilful sinners. They admit the immensely superior wisdom of the white people, and receive of their productions what they think convenient for their own purpose, but their doctrines, their faith, they will not have." [1]

Such examples could be multiplied, not only from Moffat's writings but from those of other missionaries. These men were prepared to sacrifice their pleasure, their health, their lives even, to the welfare of their people, as they conceived it. But the standards by which they judged Africans were rigid, and quite unlike any that the Africans themselves knew or subscribed to. They were not willing to study and observe the people first and to base their opinions and their policy on what they saw: they had a ready-made code, and they applied it automatically. That is why the account they gave of Africa and Africans, though it edified their readers, contributed so much less than it might have done to the better appreciation of African problems : an additional reason why, once again, though knowledge had grown, understanding had not grown in the same measure.

It is essential, in studying Livingstone's career, to keep in mind the background of thought from which it began. When he went out to Africa in 1840 he knew no more

[1] R. Moffat, *Missionary Labours and Scenes in Southern Africa* (1842), 59; *The Matabele Journals of Robert Moffat*, ed. J. P. R. Wallis (1945), i. 118-9, 293.

about it, and about its people, than his ordinary countrymen. But he very quickly picked up lessons that other,
more orthodox, missionaries never learnt; and in the
course of his career he did more than any single man to
alter the whole European conception of Africa and
Africans.

Chapter Three

Missionary Travels
(1841–1852)

THE *George* had a stormy passage out. She struck a
severe gale in the Atlantic, in which her foremast was
split, forcing her to put into Rio de Janeiro for repairs.
Livingstone took the opportunity to land, and made his
way out of the town into the Brazilian forest. It was his
first sight of a tropical landscape, and it charmed him
instantly. He was equally delighted with the simple hospitality he received. All that saddened him was the
drunkenness of English and American sailors in the
streets.

It was not until 11 March 1841 that the *George*
reached Simon's Bay. Four days later Livingstone was in
Capetown, where he had to wait some weeks before the
ship went on to Port Elizabeth, his final destination. He
stayed at Capetown with Dr. John Philip, Superintendent
of the London Missionary Society's South African
stations and the most famous man in South Africa
through his doughty and uncompromising championship
of the Africans' rights. Livingstone had received an un-
favourable account of Philip before he left England, for
Philip was an outspoken, overbearing man who made
enemies easily, and he had become involved in the sectarian and personal quarrels of the missionaries at the
Cape. But Livingstone's prejudice quickly melted away,
and he acknowledged that it had been entirely mistaken.
He found the Doctor and his wife "eminently devoted
and humble Christians". His hard words were reserved

7078

instead for the congregation of Philip's New Union Chapel : they were now engaged in an unedifying dispute with their pastor, who had just resigned his office. The words were hard indeed : "The most insolent and violent of his enemies have been raised by him from indigence to comparative affluence : several of them came to the colony with scarcely a shilling in their pockets. He took them by the hand and assisted them both by his purse, his advice and influence. Now they have their country houses, never come to chapel more than once a day and never attend a church meeting but for the purpose of ejecting the scum of their wicked hearts." There seems to have been some talk of asking Livingstone to accept the pastorate in succession to Philip; but when he preached, some of the congregation found his doctrine heterodox, and he would certainly have rejected the offer if it had been made. That was not his work, nor was he interested in such congregations.

It is worth while, however, to notice the pungency of his comments on the whole story. He was a profoundly charitable man, but one thing infallibly roused him to violent language : the squabbles of Christians, above all in the mission-field. At Capetown, at the outset of his career, he had a small taste of them. They disgusted him, and his reaction was strong. It was the same all through his life. His most tart remarks were always passed on his fellow-missionaries : he felt urgently that they had something much more important to do than to pick holes in one another, and that their work could be well done only if it were done in unity.

After a delay of about a month at the Cape, he set sail again on the last stage of his voyage. At Port Elizabeth he disembarked and began to prepare for the long journey inland to Kuruman, Moffat's station, which was to be his headquarters. It was a slow business—he left the coast on 20 May, and did not reach Kuruman until the last day of July; but he found travelling by ox-waggon an agreeable novelty, and he liked the country at once. The landscape round Port Elizabeth reminded him of Scotland, and he was glad to find that "the Hottentots are far superior in attainments to what I had expected".

He was not equally pleased with Kuruman when he arrived there. He found it indeed "a pretty spot", with a healthy climate, good gardens, and a stone-built church that was bigger than any other he had seen on a mission-station. But to him these were comparatively trifling details. What he looked for immediately was the evidence of the mission's effectiveness; and here he was dis-appointed. There seemed to be few converts. And Kuru-man, though pleasant enough in itself, was situated in a sparsely peopled region. He had not been there long before he heard that the country to the north was a good deal more densely settled, and that the single missionary who had been stationed there was being withdrawn by the Church Missionary Society, to which he belonged. At once he made up his mind that his own sphere of work lay there. He had been instructed by the Directors to await the arrival of Moffat (who was still in England) and then to move out northwards. He determined to antici-pate his orders to some extent, and in the autumn of 1841 he made a prospecting expedition with one of his senior colleagues at Kuruman, Roger Edwards.

Their journey took them some three hundred miles north-eastwards to Shokuane, which was then the capital of the Bakwena tribe and the residence of their chief, Sechele, who later became one of Livingstone's most im-portant African disciples. It initiated him into the ways of the country, but he knew that if he was really to gain an understanding of the people he would have to acquire the Sichuana language and live among them by himself. As soon as he was back at Kuruman, therefore, he began to prepare for a second journey. This time he had no white companion : he took with him only two of the mission's African converts.

He started in February 1842 and first made his way back to the Bakwena country he had visited the year before. He did not establish himself again at Shokuane, but at a village about fifteen miles to the south of it called Lepelole, which Edwards and he had fixed upon as a promising place for a new mission-station. The chief here, Bubi, a subordinate of Sechele, had received them in a very friendly way on their first visit. Livingstone now set himself to win the full confidence of the chief and his people. He quickly succeeded, and by one means in particular. In that parched country, the greatest problem was always to find water : hence the office of "rain-maker", one of the most important in the tribe. Livingstone, too, claimed to be a rain-maker, not by means of spells or charms, but through promoting irrigation, which was something new to Bubi's people. He explained the idea to the chief, who was at once struck by it and promised to furnish him with as many men as he wanted to dig the channel. In spite of a lack of the proper implements— they had one spade between them, and that had no handle —they dug a canal, four or five hundred feet long and four feet deep; and its value was understood and appreciated by the people.

Here, on the very first journey he made by himself, Livingstone's ideas stand out in contrast to those of his fellow-missionaries. Their approach to such people as the Bakwena had been all wrong, in his opinion. They had formed a settlement among them and asked leave, humbly and submissively, to instruct them. Livingstone thought their humility misplaced, and he knew their psychology was mistaken : "The missionaries solicited their permission to do what they did, and this was the very way to make them show off their airs, for they are so disobliging; if they perceive any one in the least dependent upon them, they immediately begin to tyrannise. . . . I am trying a different plan with them. I make my presence with any of them a favour, and when they show any impudence I threaten to leave them, and if they don't amend I put my threat into execution. By a bold free course among them I have not had the least difficulty in managing the most fierce."

So now, having given Bubi's people an idea of the highest practical value to them, he was careful not to make himself cheap by staying among them too long. After a month at Lepelole he moved on to the north.

The second stage of his journey might fairly be described as his first piece of African exploration, for he was travelling through country of which very little indeed was known. He had to cover much of the way on foot, since the sands of the desert through which they were advancing made it impossible to use the oxen. In this humble state, accompanied only by the two Africans from Kuruman and without any presents to ensure him a welcome, he arrived among the Bamangwato. He was hospitably received by Sekhomi, their chief, who listened with close interest to all he had to say; and when the time came for him to leave, Sekhomi sent with him one of his under-chiefs, attended by three servants, to accompany him to Kuruman and bring back a faithful report of the settlement and the people he met there.

While he was staying with Sekhomi, Livingstone paid a visit to another tribe, some twenty miles away, the Bakaa. In his *Missionary Travels* he alludes to them in a single terse sentence: "The Bakaa mountains had been visited before by a trader, who, with his people, all perished from fever." It is just like him to put it in that quiet way in his published book. What had actually happened, as he recorded in a private letter at the time, was this: the Bakaa had poisoned the food and water of the white trader, killed all his companions, eaten his oxen, stripped his waggons of their iron-work, and then burnt them. On Livingstone's approach the whole tribe fled, fearing a terrible vengeance. Only the chief and two of his men stood their ground. They were in evident terror, which vanished, significantly, when they saw Livingstone eat some porridge they prepared for him and then lie down to sleep in perfect trust. He was soon on good terms with the people, and it was to them that he preached for the first time extempore in Sichuana. When he left, the chief sent his son to escort him safely on his way. After revisiting the Bamangwato, he turned south again and made his way back to Kuruman, where he arrived in June.

As Moffat had not yet returned from England, Livingstone was still prevented from going out and establishing the new station on which his heart was fixed. Instead, he had to content himself for the moment with working in and around Kuruman. He had now somewhat modified his adverse opinion of the settlement. It had been the impulsive criticism of a young idealist, fresh from England, passed before he had any sound standards to judge by. Now he had seen the condition of some of the primitive Bechuana tribes, little touched by missions, and he began to think better of Kuruman. His first official letter to the London Missionary Society, written in July 1842, acknowledges this in handsome terms. In reply the Society, on its side, was pleased to express its formal approval of the work that Livingstone had so far performed, and to give leave at length for him to establish a new station.

When the letter containing this news arrived at Kuruman, Livingstone was once again away, on his third journey (February–June 1843). The whole Bechuana country had been disturbed in the later months of 1842 by cattle wars and by the raids of the terrible Matebele. Lepelole was no longer a possible mission-station, for Bubi and his people had been driven from it and the chief himself was dead, as the result of an unwise experiment with gunpowder. Instead, Livingstone chose another spot for his settlement, a little farther to the south : Mabotsa. As soon as he had returned to Kuruman and found the Directors' permission to go forward, he began his preparations for removal. Early in August, he and Edwards went over to Mabotsa to build a hut, and towards the end of the year they began living there.

They took with them an African convert from Kuruman, Mebalwe, to work as a teacher. Livingstone had already come to attach great importance to the use of such "native assistants", though some of his seniors regarded them doubtfully. To him it was clear that the evangelisation of Africa was far too big a task to be achieved by Europeans alone. Nor did he think that was desirable. In his opinion there were too many missionaries in South Africa already. His single journey up from Port Elizabeth had convinced him of that. At Uitenhage he found three missionaries, at Graaf Reinet five, and so on: as he bluntly told the Secretary of the Society he served, "the colonial market is literally glutted with missionaries". What obviously angered him was that they lived clustered together in these centres of civilisation instead of advancing into the unknown interior, spreading out singly, and carrying on their task with the aid of well-trained native assistants.

It is not a problem that concerns mission work alone, nor is it merely of historical interest. Very much the same choice confronts the medical service in Africa today : is it right to concentrate the main' effort on building up a few big hospitals in the main centres of population, managed by European doctors with their elaborate and careful training, or is the French system better, with its greater reliance upon a large number of dispensaries manned by African "auxiliaries" and scattered throughout the whole country? It is not a simple question, but it is one that repeatedly calls for an answer in many spheres of colonial administration.

Livingstone, at all events, had no doubt. Time and time again he urged upon the Directors of his Society the importance, the necessity, of using native assistants. Mebalwe, indeed, proved a most valuable worker, and devotedly loyal to Livingstone at a famous moment of danger. The people of Mabotsa were much worried by lions. Knowing that, if one lion is killed, the rest will generally move off at once, Livingstone determined to try to shoot one of them. He succeeded in getting to close quarters with a lion and wounding, but not killing it. As he was reloading to fire again the lion pounced on him, mauled his shoulder, and pinned him to the ground with one paw on his head. Mebalwe raised his gun courageously, but it missed fire in both barrels. The lion now sprang upon him and bit him in the thigh. Then, as he was attacking a third man, the bullets that the beast had received took effect, and he suddenly fell down dead.

Livingstone himself referred to this event very slightly in his letters home, though he was laid up for some months with the wounds that the lion had inflicted on him, and never fully recovered the use of his left arm : he suffered pain in it intermittently for the rest of his life and at any time when he attempted to raise it to the level of his shoulder. But the story quickly became legendary, and he was constantly questioned about it. Solemn people sometimes got solemn answers, given with his tongue in his cheek: to one earnest person, who asked him what he thought when the lion was holding him down, he replied, "I was thinking what part of me he would eat first". All the same, after a little reflection, he did include an account of the episode in his *Missionary Travels*, which is of great interest for its cool description of his own feelings : "The shock produced a stupor similar to that which seems to be felt by a mouse after the first shake of the cat. It caused a sort of dreaminess, in which there was no sense of pain nor feeling of terror, though quite conscious of all that was happening. . . . The shake annihilated fear, and allowed no sense of horror in looking round at the beast." The analysis is typical of his probing scientist's mind.

A few months after Livingstone had moved to Mabotsa, Moffat arrived back from England. He was of an older generation—a man now of forty-eight; and naturally his ideas centred on Kuruman, which had been largely of his making. But he, too, believed firmly in the necessity for penetrating farther inland. He had himself been twice to see Mosilikatse, the formidable chief of the Matebele, and established an ascendancy over his mind that his three subsequent visits confirmed. He had also given much of his life to an enterprise that Livingstone whole-heartedly admired : the translation of the Bible into Sichuana, which occupied him at intervals for nearly thirty years.

While he was recovering from the wounds inflicted on him by the lion, Livingstone went over to visit Moffat at Kuruman. There he fell in love with the eldest of Moffat's daughters, Mary, and became engaged to her. They were married on 2 January 1845, and returned to a new house that Livingstone had built for them at Mabotsa.

They did not occupy it for long, however. In the course of 1845 Livingstone's relations with Roger Edwards, the senior missionary who was with him, became strained and then unpleasant. It is a disagreeable story of petty jealousy. Edwards clearly looked on his colleague as a pushing youngster. He complained that Livingstone treated him as "a mere appendix", and prepared a long statement of his grievances for the Directors. He showed this document to Livingstone, who took prompt action, writing a letter home, in which he gave a full account of the whole dispute, and announcing that he would leave Mabotsa to Edwards and found a new station on his own. Edwards seems to have been taken somewhat aback at this and to have felt ashamed of himself very quickly. But Livingstone's decision was made, and he stuck to it. In the autumn of 1845 he and his wife moved on some miles farther north to Chonuane, one of the chief settlements of the Bakwena.

It meant a serious sacrifice to him, though he made nothing of that. For he had spent a good deal on building at Mabotsa, and he could ill afford to repeat the operation so soon: his salary from the Society was no more than £75 a year until his marriage, when it was raised to £100. But he had learnt his lesson. He never again tried to run a mission-station jointly with any one else.

Livingstone's residence at Chonuane, which lasted nearly two years, was important because it gave him a better opportunity than he had hitherto had to understand and become closely acquainted with an African people. The chief of the Bakwena, Sechele, was a highly intelligent man who soon showed himself sympathetic to Livingstone's ideas and prepared to go a great way towards putting them into practice. He insisted immediately on being taught to read, and he plied Livingstone constantly with shrewd, eager questions about Christianity. "On the first occasion on which I ever attempted to hold a public religious service," Livingstone records, "he remarked that it was the custom of his nation, when any new subject was brought before them, to put questions on it; and he begged me to allow him to do the same in this case. On expressing my entire willingness to answer his questions, he inquired if my forefathers knew of a future judgment. I replied in the affirmative, and began to describe the scene of 'the great white throne, and Him who shall sit on it, from whose face the heaven and earth shall flee away', etc. He said, 'You startle me—these words make all my bones to shake—I have no more strength in me; but my forefathers were living at the same time yours were, and how is it that they did not send them word about these terrible things sooner? They all passed away into darkness without knowing whither they were going.' I got out of the difficulty by explaining the geographical barriers in the North, and the gradual spread of knowledge from the South, to which we first had access by means of ships; and I expressed my belief that, as Christ had said, the whole world would yet be enlightened by the Gospel." But Sechele had not finished with the matter. He went on to object that the Kalahari Desert was a barrier too formidable to overcome : the people living to the north of it must therefore continue to remain ignorant of Christianity.

The way in which Livingstone reports this exchange is deeply characteristic of him—of his scrupulous candour ("I got out of the difficulty"), his fairness and good sense in not trying to trump Sechele's arguments with the authority of Scripture. Candour is indeed one of the most remarkable qualities of the *Missionary Travels* as a book, one of the things that contributes most to the overwhelming impression of truthfulness that it leaves on the reader's mind. Livingstone may be mistaken or outwitted, he may occasionally seem over-stern or weak : he writes everything down just as it happened, without thought of the effect it will make.

An even more remarkable example of the same thing occurs only a page or two later. He there sets out to explain the importance of the rain-maker's office, and he illustrates his explanation by a dialogue between one of them and himself. Unhappily, it is too long to quote here. It exhibits all the best traits of Livingstone's mind, including his willingness to tell a joke against himself : a genuine sense of comedy bubbles up underneath the serious intellectual argument. It is easy to see, from a passage like this, how he established his ascendancy over Africans' minds—as over those of his fellow-countrymen.

Sechele was deeply impressed by his message, and he gradually became anxious for baptism. One great difficulty stood in the way, however—a difficulty that has often been posed to missionaries in Africa and elsewhere. Sechele was a polygamist. That was not a mere matter of inclination : if it had been, the problem would have been easier to solve—at least it would have been something that concerned him alone, in his private conscience. But his public duty was involved too, for he had married daughters of three of his subordinate chiefs as a means of binding them to him and so helping to preserve the stability of his regime, which was at all times precarious. Livingstone could hardly have asked of Sechele, as chief, anything more difficult than that he should repudiate all his wives except one. But in the end he did it. After a profession of three years, "he went home, gave each of his superfluous wives new clothing, and all his own goods, which they had been accustomed to keep in their huts for him, and sent them to their parents with an intimation that he had no fault to find with them but that in parting with them he wished to follow the will of God". Not surprisingly, their parents and relatives were extremely indignant, banding together to form a powerful opposition to Sechele. But he was baptised none the less, on 1 October 1848. Later on, to Livingstone's grief, he slipped back for a time into paganism. After due repentance, he was received again as a Christian. His second conversion was permanent. More than thirty years later, when Blaikie wrote his biography of Livingstone, he was still alive, with the single wife he had retained. It is astonishing evidence of Livingstone's power over his mind that he should have been willing to make so great a sacrifice for an ideal he cannot fully have understood.

Sechele's example was not followed by his people. The Bakwena treated Livingstone with kindness and respect; they recognised him as their friend, but they noticed also that an increasingly severe drought had set in about the time of his arrival, and they naturally wondered if this had not been caused by his opposition to the traditional rain-doctors. One of them expressed the attitude of the people to him very frankly, with a blunt common sense: "To be plain with you, we should like you much better if you traded with us and then went away without for ever boring us with preaching that word of God of yours." It is like Livingstone to report this remark, in a letter to the solemn Secretary of the London Missionary Society, objectively and with perfect good humour; and like him also that he did not take his failure to convert the Bakwena too much to heart. His attitude towards them was affectionate, level-headed, and quite unemotional. He was willing to settle among them for a time, to teach them and give them all the benefits of his knowledge and skill : it was their business whether they chose to learn from him or not. He never intended to make a permanent settlement himself, among the Bakwena or any other people. That led too quickly to a life he utterly despised : the comfortable, established life of missionaries at such places as Colesberg and Grahams-town farther south, or of the Dutch clergy, secure on their £400–£500 a year. He had already decided that his life's work lay in the remote, unknown interior of Africa. It was only a matter of time, and to some extent of opportunity, before he pushed on in that direction.

Chonuane remained Livingstone's headquarters for less than two years. The gradual desiccation of the country made life there increasingly unpleasant, and in August 1847 Sechele and Livingstone abandoned it in favour of a new station situated on a river, about forty miles to the north-west, named Kolobeng. For the next five years this was Livingstone's base: a base from which, as we shall see, he was frequently absent, but the nearest thing to a settled home that he and his wife ever had. Their eldest child, Robert, had been born at Chonuane: four more followed, in 1847–1851. In after years he regretted that he did not give more time to his children while he had them with him at Kolobeng. He was busy enough indeed, building a house, supervising irrigation works, teaching the people (Sechele insisted on putting up a school for him), minister-ing to them when they were sick. He also began in these years an *Analysis of the Sichuana Language,* thirty copies of which were eventually printed in 1859. This was an original contribution to linguistic study, a true analysis, not a grammar on the old, accepted plan. A modern authority has regretted that it had so small a circulation: "It is possible", he thinks, "that, had the work been well known at the time, it would have given a great impetus to a movement away from the conventional classical gram-mar that is only now making serious progress in the realm of African linguistics." [1]

But all this work did not absor~~b~~ stone's energy. His great objective mind : he was constantly planning

---

[1] Professor A. M. Tucker of the Scho Studies in the University of London, *Livingstone the Liberator* (1940), 113 n.

L.A.—2*

afield. While he had been living at Chonuane he had made two prospecting journeys eastwards, up into the high ground on which the city of Pretoria now stands. He found the country and its people under the control of the Dutch emigrants from the Cape—the "trekkers" who had been moving north, across the Orange and Vaal rivers, for ten years past. They had expelled Mosilikatse and his Matebele from the country in 1839, and claimed it by right of conquest for themselves. They also claimed the services of the inhabitants, which they exacted on terms that differed little from a mild form of slavery. The main reason why they had arrived in this country at all was a dislike of the new humanitarian policy of the British government at the Cape and a vehement hatred of Dr. Philip and the London Missionary Society, whom they held responsible for inspiring it. Naturally, therefore, they looked on Livingstone with mistrust. He was an agent of the same Society; and he was living on terms of suspicious friendliness with a chief of the Bakwena. Moreover, Sechele's territory lay in an important strategic position, athwart what was already recognised as the likely highway into the interior—the "Road to the North" that has played such a vital part in the modern history of South Africa. It was not to be expected that Livingstone should be welcomed by the Boer farmers, but they treated him with civility, and agreed, on his representations, to abandon, or at any rate postpone, a projected attack on Sechele, designed to deprive his people of the firearms they were thought to possess. (The Boers believed they already mustered 500 guns : Livingstone—who should have known—said the real number was five.) But that was the total measure of his success.

These visits made one thing perfectly clear to him : no field for his missionary work was open here. If he wished to move out into unknown territory, it must be across the lahari Desert. "All my desires tend forwards, to the " he wrote in June 1848. ". . . Why, we have a

world before us here. We have no missionary beyond this
—all is dark."

Livingstone's interest in this country, as a missionary,
coincided with Sechele's, which was of a different kind.
Sechele knew that ivory was secured there, in large
quantities: he wished to share in the profits of the trade.
He was also anxious to visit a great chief, Sebituane, who
lived far away to the north, by a great lake. Sebituane
had saved his life in infancy, and Sechele always thought
of him with veneration. Livingstone secured other help,
too. During his residence in Bechuanaland he had more
than once met English big-game hunters—Captain Steele
and Major Vardon of the Indian Army and William
Cotton Oswell, a civilian in the East India Company's
service. Hearing now of Livingstone's projected journey
to the north, into this vast ivory country, Oswell determined to join him, bringing with him another friend,
Mungo Murray. Oswell was a man of wealth, a generous
and self-effacing character, who made an important contribution to Livingstone's work. It is clear that, in his
simple, direct way, he admired the missionary deeply.
Livingstone had a very high regard for him, too. Again
and again he acknowledges his generosity: he records, and
endorses, the Africans' admiration for Oswell's courage—
it was his practice to hunt big game on foot, without dogs,
dependent solely on his own skill in each contest with
rhinoceros or elephant.

Livingstone's plan was to strike out northwards until
he reached the lake that was said to lie away in the interior. Sechele, in the end, decided not to go with him, for
fear of a Boer attack on his people while he was away.
But he gave him all the help he could, and Oswell hired
the guides. They set off on 1 June 1849, accompanied,
as a matter of course, by Mrs. Livingstone and the
children.

The shortest route to the lake was impracticable, for
it meant crossing the most arid part of the Kalahari
Desert: a way had to be taken that skirted the desert's

eastern edge. It has often been pointed out, by writers from Livingstone onwards, that the Kalahari is by no means a complete desert. Though it has no running water, rain does sometimes fall there (and when it does it stands for months in the sun-baked hollows), and water can often be found by sinking wells. Nor is this "desert" without vegetation : water-melons and red cucumbers grow in it, together with a few other edible plants.

But when all has been said in its defence, the Kalahari —even its eastern fringe, which Livingstone was now crossing—is a tract of most inhospitable country. The travellers' task was made more difficult through the opposition of Sekhomi, the chief of the Bamangwato, a distant and junior relative of Sechele. Sechele had done what he could to smooth this away in advance, sending two formal requests to Sekhomi to allow Livingstone's party to pass, accompanied each time by the *douceur* of an ox. But Sekhomi refused. His stated reason was that he was afraid the Matebele would attack and kill Livingstone, and if that happened he would be held responsible by the British government. In fact, he seems really to have been moved by the wish to defend his share in the handsome profits of the ivory trade. When Livingstone moved north, defying his disapproval, he put all the obstacles he could in the white man's path, sending his own men to drive away any Bushmen who might assist the party and to spread rumours that Livingstone was bent on plunder. In spite of these hindrances, however, and of a dangerously slow progress that worried their guide, they reached the River Zouga, which was reported to run into the lake, on 4 July. They had now only to follow the course of the river : the hardest part of their task was done. Presently the Zouga was joined by another river, the Tamanakle, flowing in from the north-east. "I inquired whence it came," wrote Livingstone. " 'Oh, from a country full of rivers—so many no one can tell their number—and full of large trees !' This was the first confirmation of statements I had heard from the Bakwains who had been with Sebituane, that the country beyond was not 'the large sandy plateau' of the philosophers. The prospect of a highway capable of being traversed by boats to an entirely unexplored and very populous region grew from that time forward stronger and stronger in my mind; so much so that, when we actually came to the lake, this idea occupied such a large portion of my mental vision that the actual discovery seemed of but little importance." The finding of the Tamanakle marks another stage in Livingstone's career, leading him on to his next great venture, to the Zambesi.

It was on 1 August 1849—exactly two months after they had left Kolobeng—that Livingstone and his companions, first among Europeans, stood on the edge of Lake Ngami. As they looked across it they could see no farther shore. From what the inhabitants of the country told him, Livingstone estimated that its circumference must be at least seventy miles. But it was very shallow, and its water fell markedly in the dry season. It was plain, too, that the volume of water in the lake was growing less. In the century since Livingstone discovered it, desiccation has gone much further. Ngami is no longer marked as a lake on our maps today, merely as a large swamp, though in the rainy season its bed continues to fill, even if only for a short time. Livingstone recognised that whatever importance his discovery might have from a geographical point of view, it was not likely to be of much commercial value. His determination to press on into the alleged land of rivers to the north was fortified.

So far he had fulfilled only one of the objects of his journey. He had found the lake, but he had not yet seen Sebituane, who lived a considerable distance beyond it. Here, however, he found himself balked by a young chief who refused to give him the guides he asked for. The season was now well advanced, and Livingstone decided, with regret, to return to Kolobeng.

Next year he made another attempt to reach Sebituane, but was defeated through an outbreak of fever among his family and servants. It was on this journey that he first made acquaintance with a new danger—the tsetse-fly. The tsetse, which has played so great a part in the modern history of tropical Africa, had become known to scientists only within the previous twenty years; the first specimens had been brought to England by Major Vardon from the Limpopo, away to the south-east, in 1848. Livingstone knew little of the poisonous properties of its bite, but he soon learnt that it was fatal to oxen, horses, and dogs. Here was another formidable difficulty in the way of opening up a route to the interior.

A third effort to reach Sebituane was made in 1851, once again in the company of Oswell. Beyond Lake Ngami the party came to a terrifying stretch of desert— "the only vegetation was a low scrub in deep sand; not a bird or insect enlivened the landscape"—and they began to suffer seriously from the lack of water. Livingstone has recorded something of the agony of his mind and his wife's as they watched their children's thirst increase. It was only after four days of dreadful suspense that water was found.

Thereafter their difficulties eased, and they were conducted by an effective though ill-favoured guide ("the most like the ugly negro of the tobacconists' shops I ever saw") to the country of Sebituane's people, the Makololo. Livingstone and Oswell then went on ahead, down the River Chobe in a canoe. They found the great chief had come a hundred miles to meet them. It had been the highest ambition of his life to see a white man. This was the crowning moment of his career, and he gave Livingstone a generous welcome.

That career had indeed been a remarkable one. On the surface it looks merely like a life of successful warfare, one that could be paralleled a dozen times over among his contemporaries. But just as the character and ideas of Mosilikatse, as they have lately been revealed to us in Moffat's journals, show him to have been something altogether bigger than the mere murderous robber he appears at first sight, so in Sebituane Livingstone discerned qualities of heart and mind that lifted him above the common race of African tyrants. "He was decidedly the best specimen of a native chief I ever met", Livingstone wrote in 1857; and there is no reason to suppose he would have altered that verdict if he had been writing at the end of his life. He did not bestow such praise lightly. Though he loved Africans and felt a deep sympathy with them, Livingstone regarded them unsentimentally, judging them by the same standards of humanity, honour, and justice as those that he applied to other men. He devotes five pages of the *Missionary Travels* to a biographical sketch of Sebituane, in which he brings out the chief's simple valour ("unlike Mosilikatse, Dingaan, and others, he always led his men into battle himself"), his tenacity in defeat, his mercifulness, and his affability even to humble strangers. By his own efforts alone he had welded the Makololo together until they had become powerful enough to stand up to the Matebele on equal terms. They occupied a territory with something like natural frontiers —the Zambesi on the north, the desert and the Chobe on the south, and plenty of readily defensible positions in its swamps; their political life was at least as stable as that of any of their neighbours : all this they owed in the first place to their chief Sebituane.

It is clear that Sebituane, on his side, was not disappointed with the white man now he had met him. He opened his heart to Livingstone and offered him the choice of any part of his own country to settle in. Livingstone was prepared to resume his missionary work for a time, leaving Oswell to explore the country farther up to the Zambesi. But just as things began to seem so hopeful the situation changed. Sebituane fell ill of inflammation of the lungs. Livingstone knew his life was in danger, but dared not treat him, lest if the chief died the blame should fall on him. Though that was only common prudence, it must have cost him a great effort of restraint to sit by and

37

watch without intervening. He began to unfold his message, to speak of a life after death. But it was too late. Before he could make any real progress, Sebituane died. Livingstone's comment is touching, and it shows how far away he already stood from the narrow, bleak Calvinism of his youth : "I never felt so much grieved by the loss of a black man before; and it was impossible not to follow him in thought into the world of which he had just heard before he was called away, and to realise somewhat of the feelings of those who pray for the dead."

Sebituane's death might have been disastrous for Livingstone. But the succession devolved quietly on one of his daughters, Mamochisane, and she confirmed her father's permission to Livingstone to settle where he chose. Oswell and he then went on north-eastwards, on a prospecting journey; and at the end of June 1851 they reached the Zambesi at Sesheke. This was the second important geographical discovery they had made. The earlier Portuguese maps had represented the river as rising much farther to the east. But its discovery meant something more to Livingstone than a change on the map. It offered him the hope of a new entrance into the country direct from the west or east coast of Africa, independent of the Boers, and by a route perhaps more hospitable than that over the Kalahari Desert.

One further discovery Livingstone also made here, of the highest importance. On their way up to the river they were met by a number of Makololo wearing bright new cottons and calico and baize. It appeared that these goods had been bought, in exchange for boys, from a people called the Mambari, who lived in Portuguese Angola, to the west. This slave trade had begun only the year before. The Makololo had disliked the idea of it at first. But the Mambari had been able to offer them not only clothes but guns in exchange for the boys, and the temptation was too strong for their scruples. A little later, on a raid to the eastward, the Makololo came into touch with some

Portuguese traders.[1] They, too, had guns to sell : three English muskets purchased thirty of the prisoners the Makololo had taken on their foray.

Discussing this business with Oswell, Livingstone came to form what can be said to be one of the cardinal principles of policy on which the rest of his life's work was based : "If the slave-market were supplied with articles of European manufacture by legitimate commerce, the trade in slaves would become impossible. It seemed more feasible to give the goods, for which the people now part with their servants, in exchange for ivory and other products of the country, and thus prevent the trade at the beginning, than try to put a stop to it at any of the subsequent steps. This could be effected only by establishing a highway from the coast into the centre of the country." These were not new ideas. He had himself attended, in his student days in London, the great meeting at Exeter Hall that launched the Niger Expedition of 1841 on just those principles. The Niger Expedition had been a disaster. But that was from foolish planning. Its failure did not invalidate the ideas on which it rested, and Livingstone devoted most of his life, from now on, to the prosecution of "Christianity and commerce", the ousting of the slave trade by "legitimate" trade.

The immediate need was quite clear. Before this policy could be shaped further or implemented, it was essential to learn more about the Zambesi basin, its peoples, and the slave trade in which they were becoming involved. Livingstone could achieve this in only one way : by exploring the country himself, ranging freely along the valley of the great river and up into the unknown heart of the continent. It was an extension of the work he had been doing for the past two years, but so great an extension as to change his function entirely and the conditions

[1] This is what Livingstone says in a letter written at the time (1 October 1851 : *Some Letters from Livingstone,* ed. Chamberlin, 152). In *Missionary Travels,* 92, he speaks of them as "Arabs from Zanzibar".

in which he would be working. For the moment he would become—at least in appearance—an explorer first and foremost, and only incidentally a missionary. That raised an important question with his employers, the London Missionary Society. Would they sanction the change? In a long letter, dated 17 October 1851, he laid his case before the Secretary of the Society, Dr. Tidman. After expounding his view of the importance of the journey he outlined, he went on to offer himself for the service, at the same time setting out all the arguments for and against his going.

One of the chief obstacles in his way was a domestic problem. He estimated that this new task would take two years, and he had reluctantly come to the conclusion that if he went he could not take his family with him. Hitherto they had accompanied him on all his journeys, sharing his hardships and dangers. But his wife's health had suffered severely, particularly after the birth of her fourth child at Kolobeng in 1850 and its death at the age of six weeks. As soon as she heard that he was contemplating this new journey, so much longer and potentially more dangerous than the rest, his mother-in-law wrote a firm letter, insisting that he should leave his family behind. He had already been frequently criticised for taking them with him. Much of this criticism was purely ill-natured, coming from people who were jealous of his achievement and thought this a suitable pretext for blackening his character. And it is important to remember that Mary Livingstone herself was determined to stay with him. Oswell records her courage and her devotion as a wife, adding that he "saw her fail on one occasion only—when her husband wanted to leave her behind". There was, too, a further problem. If he left them, where was he to leave them? Kolobeng was too precarious a station. He could not plant them on the Moffats at Kuruman. The best thing appeared to be to send them home. That would make it possible to put the elder children to school—Robert was now six; and Mary would be enabled to re-

cover her health completely, as she could hardly expect
to do if she remained in Africa. The last difficulty was the
financial one. Livingstone certainly could not afford to
support his family at home as well as himself in the field,
on a salary (already sadly overdrawn) of £100 a year. He
could not manage even to find the capital outlay required
for clothing them in a manner suitable for their return to
England.

All these problems, however, were solved. The Directors of the London Missionary Society approved Livingstone's plan and undertook to maintain his family at
home while he was on his travels. It was a large-minded
decision, always to be remembered in their favour. For
they can have understood only very imperfectly the real
importance of the plans that Livingstone had formed;
the Society was not rich; and there were plenty of people,
as Livingstone himself knew, ready to impugn his motives,
to attack him for abandoning his calling as a missionary
in favour of the worldly success to be achieved as an explorer. All in all, then, it can be said that the Society
behaved generously by Livingstone at this critical
moment.

In the winter of 1851–1852 he travelled down to the
Cape with his family. The problem of their clothing was
met by the generosity of Oswell, who insisted on fitting
them out for their journey himself, at a total expense of
£170. Thus equipped, they sailed for home in the
Trafalgar on 23 April 1852.

Livingstone spent the next six weeks in Capetown, preparing for his journey. He had to meet a good deal of
suspicion on the part of the government. It was a delicate
juncture in the development of its policy towards the
Boers and the Africans in the interior. In January 1852
the Sand River Convention had been signed, by which
the British government recognised the independence of
the Transvaal, and undertook not to form any alliances
with "the coloured nations north of the Vaal River". This
was part of a resolute policy of withdrawal from the

41

affairs of the South African interior, pressed upon the government at home by Cobden and the anti-imperialists. It could not be effected without disappointing, even betraying, allies who had previously counted on British assistance. The policy had been vocally criticised by the missionaries at the Cape, and Livingstone did not disguise his opinion that it was wrong. Accordingly, when he set about trying to purchase the ammunition he needed for his journey, government officials put every possible obstacle in his way, suspecting that it was really his intention to arm the African chiefs against the Boers of the Transvaal. Deeply though he sympathised with the Africans, above all with Sechele, the suspicion was unjust. In any case, he had not the money to lay out in this way, even if he had wanted to. His own equipment cost him all that he could afford.

His stay at Capetown, then, was a gloomy one, newly separated as he was from his family and vexed by official obstruction. But, characteristically, he turned it to good account. While he was waiting he put himself under the tuition of Thomas Maclear, the Astronomer Royal at the Cape, to enable him to take accurate and satisfactory observations of his course as he travelled. Maclear became his friend and constant correspondent, and Livingstone attributed much of the accuracy of his own work as a geographer to him : "The promise he made on parting, that he would examine and correct all my observations, had more effect in making me persevere in overcoming the difficulties of an unassisted solitary observer, than anything else; so whatever credit may be attached to the geographical positions laid down in my route, must be attributed to the voluntary aid of the excellent and laborious astronomer of the Cape Observatory."

Furnished at length with the ammunition he needed and fortified by his lessons from Maclear, he left Capetown on his northward journey on 8 June 1852.

Chapter Four

The First Great Journey
(1852–1856)

THE first stages of the journey were extremely tedious.
Livingstone had six Africans with him and a fair
quantity of baggage, together with goods consigned to
people who lay on his route. He therefore travelled in a
lumbering Cape waggon, hauled by ten oxen. In retrospect he did his best to make light of the tedium, describing the method of travel as "a prolonged system of
picknicking, excellent for the health, and agreeable to
those who are not over fastidious about trifles, and who
delight in being in the air". But to him, anxious to get to
grips with the great problems that lay ahead, it must have
been a weary business. He occupied himself with his study
of the Sichuana language, and even began to compile a
dictionary of it : "I did not know I had so many words in
my head as I have put down," he wrote, "but every time
I sit down there is no end to them. They are hooked together by strange associations."

After suffering various minor accidents, towards the
end of August one of the wheels of his waggon broke, and
it was only slowly and with difficulty that it was dragged
on to Kuruman. There he found Moffat engaged in
carrying his Sichuana Bible through the press. It was not
his intention to stay long, but he was held up by the repairs to his waggon, which took a fortnight.

It is not surprising that he should have come in the end
to regard these repeated delays, which seemed so tiresome
at the time, as providential. For while he was at Kuru-

man, Sechele's wife arrived with a letter from her husband for Moffat, announcing that he had been savagely attacked by the Boers. They had demanded that he should acknowledge their overlordship and that he should stop the English and Griquas from travelling northwards through his territory. He refused, whereupon the Boers opened fire on his capital. They killed sixty of his people, removed many more into captivity, and plundered and burnt the town. They also took special care to loot and destroy Livingstone's house at Kolobeng, eight miles to the north. On his side, Sechele claimed that his people had killed thirty-eight of the Boers. The assault occurred on 27 August. If Livingstone had not been delayed by the accidents to his waggon, he would have been there by that time, and in that case there is little doubt that he would have been killed; some of the Boers, indeed, were said to have remarked that they had intended his death.

The motive for the attack was clear enough. Sechele was alleged to be sheltering a chief called Moselele, who was said to have committed several murders in the Transvaal, and to have refused point-bank to give him up, remarking, "Who wants Moselele can come and fetch him out of my stomach". If these were really Sechele's words, they could be construed only as a challenge, which the Boers were happy to take up. Their animus against Livingstone arose from their belief that he was responsible for supplying Sechele with arms; and the party that was detached to destroy his house stated that they found there "a complete workshop for repairing guns, and a quantity of materials of war which Livingstone was storing for Sechele".

This episode has been long and hotly discussed, by Livingstone himself, and from the Boer side by P. E. Scholtz, one of the leaders of the raid, and Paul Kruger, who served on it as a young field-cornet.[1] There is

[1] See *Missionary Travels*, 133–6; R. J. Campbell, *Livingstone* (1929), 145–51; *Some Letters from Livingstone*, ed. Chamberlin

no sound evidence whatever that Livingstone supplied Sechele with arms, and all probability is against it. The "complete workshop for repairing guns" was surely something much more modest and quite innocuous. The big-game hunters who passed that way had all left goods at Livingstone's house at Kolobeng. They may well have left a few guns there, too, and some simple apparatus for repairing them. If this was so, it is easy to see how Scholtz and his friends, excited by the attack and under the necessity of justifying it, may have exaggerated several times over what they found.

Livingstone lost no time in writing off to Lieutenant-Governor Darling to acquaint him with the story. "The first blow has been struck by the Boers," he wrote, "and that, too, on a tribe which has never given them the smallest provocation, nor for the last eight years at least the slightest trouble to any of its neighbours." In the same letter he took occasion to mention his own losses, which he put at £335—a very substantial sum to him at that time. It is not to be wondered at that he got no redress. His demand was a test of the British government's determination to uphold the Sand River Convention, signed only eight months before. The very purpose of the agreement had been to enable Britain to withdraw from the imprecise responsibilities she had assumed north of the Vaal. Livingstone's complaint related to matters that no longer concerned her.

There is nothing to show that he was disappointed at this failure. If he understood the nature of the Sand

(1940), 178–80; J. A. I. Agar-Hamilton, *The Road to the North* (1937), 20, 80–1; *The Memoirs of Paul Kruger* (1902), 42–5. It is hard to reconcile Kruger's positive statement, made in old age in his *Memoirs,* that Livingstone was supplying arms and ammunition to Sechele, with his remark to General Smuts that Gordon Cumming was the gun-runner, and that the accusation against Livingstone proved to be erroneous: J. C. Smuts, *Africa and some World Problems* (1930), 6. Professor E. A. Walker's view (*A History of South Africa,* 1935 ed., 289 n.) that the whole attack on Livingstone's house was hardly more than a bit of horseplay seems to me strangely unconvincing.

River Convention, he cannot have expected any result from his protest. But however philosophically he might put up with his loss, the attack on Sechele seriously affected his plans. The raid confirmed Livingstone's earlier view that the opening-up of the Zambesi basin could not be undertaken from the south by the route he was at present following. The Boers had made it clear, by the demand they had made to Sechele, that they intended to close the "Road to the North" that skirted the Kalahari Desert, if they could. Hence it was now more important than ever that the whole course of the Zambesi should be carefully examined, to discover practicable routes of approach from the east or the west. It was therefore particularly galling for Livingstone to be detained for three months at Kuruman, when he was desperately anxious to press on with all the speed he could make. But the Boer raid had made it almost impossible for him to secure servants for his northward journey : the Bakwena were naturally afraid of advancing into country where they might be attacked as Sechele and his people had been. It was not until 20 November that he was able to start, in company with a half-caste West Indian named George Fleming, who was on his way to open up trade with the Makololo. They had six servants between them: "The worst possible specimens of those who imbibe the vices without the virtues of Europeans; but we had no choice and were glad to get away on any terms."

A day or two out from Kuruman they met Sechele, travelling southward with the firm intention of going to England and laying his wrongs before Queen Victoria in person. He tried hard to get Livingstone to go with him; but failure did not deter him, and he went on his way. He got as far as Capetown, and then was forced to return home through lack of money for the voyage.

For fear of encountering the Boers, Livingstone and Fleming took a route somewhat west of the usual one, which brought them at times within the desert itself. Their original servants, as might be expected, left them, but they managed to secure others in their place, and without any undue difficulty they reached Linyanti on 23 May 1853. The Makololo gave them a great welcome, the entire population of the town—six or seven thousand people—coming out to see the waggons in motion.

Since their previous visit an important political change had taken place. Mamochisane had abdicated in favour of her brother Sekeletu and, and after some discussion, he had been accepted as chief. But there was a second brother, Mpepe, who had been entrusted with some power during the lifetime of his father, Sebituane; and he now, inevitably, put himself forward as leader of the opposition. He allied himself with the slave-traders, whom Livingstone had found just making their way into the country on his previous visit. The situation was a common one, the slave-traders allying with one party in the state, hoping for civil war and a share in the captives taken. In this case they thought they might do even better, for Mpepe planned to kill his brother and secure the chieftainship for himself: if that happened, the slave-traders would enjoy the friendship of the ruler of this large and powerful people. He lost no time, making two attempts on Sekeletu's life immediately after Livingstone's arrival. The second of them failed because Livingstone unwittingly placed his body between Sekeletu's and Mpepe. The same night Sekeletu struck : his brother was quietly executed. For the moment the political situation at Linyanti was precarious; but it soon appeared that Sekeletu was powerful enough to maintain his position, and Mpepe's faction was broken up.

Sekeletu was only a young man of eighteen, and he had little of his father's remarkable quality of heart and mind. But Livingstone liked him, and he respected his candour. When he tried to press Christianity on him, Sekeletu said he did not wish to learn to read the Bible, lest it "might change his heart, and make him content with only one wife, like Sechele". He announced, firmly and frankly,

47

that he wanted always to have five wives at least.

A week after his arrival at Linyanti, Livingstone had the first attack of fever he had suffered on this journey. He at once called in a Makololo doctor, thinking that he might have some well-tried remedy that was more efficient than those of Europeans. But the hope was vain, and he cured himself in his own way. Livingstone tells us little, in general, about his illnesses, on a settled principle, which he stated a little later on : "I am already getting tired of quoting my fevers, and never liked to read travels myself where much was said about the illnesses of the traveller." In reading the published accounts of his first two journeys, one must always bear this reticence in mind. On the last journey it is different. Sickness takes a constant and leading part in the *Last Journals,* partly in its own right as one of the main elements in the story, partly because the journals were printed, after his death, very much as they were written, whereas the first two expeditions were described by Livingstone himself in books compiled afterwards on the basis of the notes he made at the time. In the process of compilation, most of the tale of his own illness and hardships disappeared.

Livingstone's first objective in the Makololo country was to prospect for a site suitable for a mission-station healthy enough for Europeans to live in. Sekeletu agreed to provide him with the transport he needed, and decided to join in the prospecting himself. They set off at the end of June, travelling overland to Sesheke, and then ascending the Zambesi through the country of the Barotse. It was a large expedition—160 men, in a fleet of thirty-three canoes. Livingstone was deeply impressed by the Zambesi, often more than a mile wide and studded with large islands, which "at a little distance seem great rounded masses of sylvan vegetation reclining on the bosom of the glorious stream. The beauty of the scenery of some of the islands is greatly increased by the date-palm, with its gracefully curved fronds and refreshing light-green colour . . . and the lofty palmyra towering far above, and casting its feathery foliage against a cloudless sky." But though the river was large its course was impeded by rapids : at the Falls of Gonye the canoes had to be taken out of the water and carried a mile overland. They met some Portuguese half-castes at Naliele, who had made their way across from the west coast. But there was no trace whatever of any previous visit to the country by a white man, either within living memory or in the traditions of the people.

A little higher up the river they encountered the tsetse-fly, and Livingstone knew that it was useless to pursue his search for a healthy station farther. There was nothing for it but to return to Linyanti.

The immediate object of the expedition had not been achieved, but Livingstone would not abandon the ultimate purpose that lay beyond. This failure made it more than ever necessary to try to open up a way to the coast, and that he determined to embark on without any further delay. The experience of living with the Makololo at such close quarters had made a deep impression on his mind. "Nine weeks' intimate intercourse—hearing their conversation, anecdotes, quarrelling, roaring, dancing, singing, and murdering, have imparted a greater disgust at heathenism than I ever had before." It led him to decide that he had greatly underestimated the latent effect of the missions in the south. They might make few formal converts, but he now saw that their teaching and example were having a profound influence on the people who came into contact with them. These indirect consequences, he concluded, were "worth all the money and labour that have been expended to produce them". The point is an important one, and Livingstone was certainly right, as any candid student of African history—whether he subscribes to the religious objects of missions or not—must agree.

His remarks on the degradation of paganism were not meant to reflect unfavourably on the kindness of his hosts. He recognised that Sekeletu had done all he could to help

49

him, and he wrote of the people as "these (to me at least) very confiding and affectionate Makololo". His experiences among them had served only to give a new sense of urgency to his quest. And when he announced his proposal to travel to the west coast, he found a keen interest in the project among the Makololo themselves, who were much taken with the idea of developing a trade with Europeans by this means. They genuinely wished it to be a "legitimate" trade, and not a trade in slaves. The idea of the slave trade had indeed been quite unknown to the Makololo until it had been introduced to them, at the time of Livingstone's visits, by Portuguese half-castes and their African allies, the Mambari, and by Arabs from Zanzibar. They wanted to exchange their ivory for cloth, on terms more favourable than they could get from the African middlemen to the west and the agents of the Cape traders to the south. Accordingly, they appointed a band of twenty-seven men to accompany Livingstone on his journey. They were not in his employment : they went at the express order of Sekeletu. And though they have always been referred to as "Makololo", by Livingstone himself and by all his biographers, in fact only two of them were of that people : the rest were Barotse and men of other neighbouring tribes.

On this occasion, as usual, Livingstone travelled light. He gives us an inventory of his goods and equipment. "The outfit was rather spare," he remarks, "and intended to be still more so when we should come to leave the canoes." A large baggage train would make his journey slower and expose him to plunder on the way.

The expedition left Linyanti on 11 November 1853. For the first six weeks they were going again over the route traversed with Sekeletu. Their routine, as long as they kept to the canoes, was always the same. They rose at five, drank coffee, packed up, and embarked, paddling on until about eleven, when they took a small meal and an hour's rest : then on again, until two hours before sunset, when they would choose a place of encampment and prepare whatever evening meal might be available. The fire was the centre of the camp, and Livingstone's very small tent would be set up four or five feet away from it. The men, dividing themselves up according to their tribes, would then run up little sheds for themselves, with a framework of poles and a covering of long grasses. The oxen, which liked the fire, would be given a place near it, and in less than an hour the whole company would be at rest. "It was a picturesque sight at night," wrote Livingstone, "when the clear bright moon of these climates glances on the sleeping forms around, to look out upon the attitudes of profound repose both men and beasts assume. There being no danger from wild animals in such a night, the fires are allowed almost to go out . . . the picture was one of perfect peace."

His observations of the country led him to form great hopes for its future development. The banks of the river were well populated, and if a regular system of porterage could be instituted at the points where its course was interrupted by rapids, it would be possible "to make it equal to our canals for hundreds of miles". The soil appeared to be rich, and if ploughed up instead of being left to produce rank vegetation, the country could, he thought, be made very fertile. Livingstone has proved over-sanguine about the prospects of the Zambesi valley. It was not his observation that was at fault, however, but his estimate of the incentives to improvement.

Some weeks after leaving Linyanti, they arrived at a confluence of two great rivers. Livingstone believed that the river flowing in from the east, known as the Kabompo, was really the main Zambesi : that from the north he noted as the Leeba. He therefore thought that at this point, by sailing up the Leeba, he was leaving the Zambesi. Modern geographers have determined that the "Leeba" is the main stream, the Zambesi, and the Kabompo a tributary. The valley here begins to narrow, running up towards the watershed that divides the valleys of the Zambesi, the Coanza to the west, and the Kasai to the north. Shortly afterwards they were obliged to abandon their canoes and continue their journey by land, struggling often through dense forest. They were continually in drenching rain, which, as usual, brought fever with it. Livingstone's only comment was that, for all these discomforts, there was a pleasure in the change of scenery, utterly unlike the perpetual glare of the Kalahari, in which he had lived so long; and the incessant rain still delighted him after the terrible drought of the desert.

None the less, his contented, quiet cheerfulness could not remove the hardships he and his followers were beginning to endure. They were frequently short of food, and from time to time they were in physical danger. The Makololo, like the Matebele and the Zulus, were greatly feared and disliked by their neighbours. Livingstone had to live down his connection with them before he could overcome the suspicions of the people whose country they were traversing. They were starting, moreover, to enter the zone of the slave-traders operating from Portuguese territory to the west; and that, as always, increased the people's hostility to strangers. And when they secured a welcome, that slowed up their progress, too : for these people had never set eyes on a white man before, and each ruler considered it a matter of credit to keep his strange guest as long as he could.

His dealings with these chiefs were characteristically straightforward. He told them exactly what it was he was trying to do, undeterred by the knowledge that his objects must have been totally incomprehensible to every one he met. "I have always been satisfied", he wrote, "that, even though there were no other considerations, the truthful way of dealing with the uncivilised is unquestionably the best." But it is worth remembering that other travellers, no less honest than Livingstone, adopted a different practice. Mary Kingsley, for instance, records: "I find I get on best among the unadulterated Africans in the guise of a trader; there is something reasonable about trade to all men, and you see the advantage of it is that, when you first appear among people who have never seen anything like you before, they naturally regard you as a devil; but when you want to buy or sell with them, they recognise there is something human and reasonable about you. . . . The trading method enables you to sit as an honoured guest at faraway inland village fires; it enables you to become the confidential friend of that ever-powerful factor in all human societies, the old ladies." [1]

The rulers through whose territories Livingstone passed as he ascended the river were none of them great or very strong. He encountered no people as powerful as the Makololo. The political units here were smaller, though all the Balonda, who lived on the upper Zambesi, owed some kind of allegiance to a chief named Matiamvo, away to the north-east. The most considerable ruler Livingstone met was Shinte, who received them at his capital with a good deal of ceremony in the presence of a thousand of his people and three hundred warriors. He treated them kindly, bestowing food on them and promising to furnish them with guides "who knew all the paths which led to the white men". Shinte himself had never seen a white man before. But two Portuguese half-castes were at his town when Livingstone arrived, with a chain-gang of enslaved women—to the horror of his men, who were not accustomed to such things : " 'They are not men,' they exclaimed (meaning they are beasts), 'who treat their children so !' " It was indeed evident that Shinte was well acquainted with the ideas and methods of the slave-traders. Thinking to please him, one night he presented Livingstone with a slave-girl, aged about ten, remarking that it was his custom to bestow a child upon his visitors. When Livingstone declined the present, Shinte merely supposed he had done so because the girl was too small, and promptly sent for a bigger one to take her place. He found it impossible to understand why this offer too was refused. He did everything in his power to express the pleasure that Livingstone's visit gave him, and

[1] S. Gwynn, *The Life of Mary Kingsley* (2nd ed., 1933), 101.

parted with him after ten days with the utmost reluctance. On the night before he left he came into Livingstone's tent, looked over all its contents with intense
interest and then, "closing the tent, so that none of his
own people might see the extravagance of which he was
about to be guilty, he drew out from his clothing a string
of beads, and the end of a conical shell, which is considered, in regions far from the sea, of as great value as
the Lord Mayor's badge is in London. He hung it round
my neck and said, 'There, now you *have* a proof of my
friendship'."

Though Shinte dispatched them with a supply of food,
they were soon hungry again and obliged to live mainly
on manioc porridge, which Livingstone likened to starch
made from diseased potatoes. One chief alone, Katema,
seems to have understood their plight and set himself to
feed them up. At their first introduction to him, he produced sixteen baskets of meal, six fowls, and a dozen eggs,
said how sorry he was to learn that they had been hungry
the previous night and humanely dismissed them at once,
saying : "Go home, and cook and eat, and you will then
be in a fit state to speak to me, at an audience I will give
you tomorrow." After this discerning generosity, Livingstone's sly comment on his appearance reads most un-
kindly : "He looked as if he had fallen asleep tipsy, and
dreamed of his greatness."

They were now crossing the watershed, skirting the
southern fringes of Lake Dilolo. Livingstone thinks it
proper to explain why he did not turn aside to examine
the lake, which was said never to have been visited by
any of the traders. Owing to fever, he had eaten nothing
at all for two days and had spent the nights drinking great
draughts of water : he felt it was his duty, and certainly
as much as he could manage, to press straight on his way.
At last they were able to take a westerly course, after the
long northward climb up the Zambesi valley. Livingstone
could feel that at any rate they were now heading directly
for the sea. As they advanced, they found more and more

evidence of the slave trade, and the price commonly asked for the food the travellers bought was gunpowder. On 27 February they crossed the Kasai ("a most beautiful river, and very much like the Clyde in Scotland"), and five weeks of extremely unpleasant travelling began. Hitherto they had encountered delays and arguments with the chiefs whose territories they had passed through, but little open hostility. Here they found no friendly welcome anywhere—nothing but constantly exorbitant demands. As they moved farther west, the formula became stereotyped : if they wanted food, they must pay for it with "a man, an ox, or a gun". Livingstone constantly explained that "my men might as well give me as I give one of them, for we were all free men". Their guns were too precious to spare. As for oxen, they were precious too, for riding as well as for food; but they did from time to time part with one of them, until they had only three left. In consequence, they were hungrier than ever before, especially as they were passing through a country where the diet of the people was meagre : moles and mice provided most of the flesh that was ordinarily eaten.

On 4 March they entered the territory of the Chiboque, who, as they subsequently discovered, bore the reputation of being the most savage and inhospitable people in the whole of this country. Their reputation was certainly well deserved, to judge by Livingstone's experience of them. He had a tense encounter with them at Njambi. After an exchange in which his present was scorned and the usual demands made, Livingstone and his party were surrounded by Chiboque, who were heard to observe with contempt : "They have only five guns." The ground of complaint against the visitors was that one of them had, in spitting, allowed a little saliva to fall on the legs of one of the Chiboque. The two men had been engaged in an apparently friendly conversation before this episode, and the offender had done his best to apologise. But the alleged insult provided an excuse for plunder too good to be missed. Livingstone tried to make amends by giving the chief a shirt, to which he afterwards added some beads and a large handkerchief. But these presents were merely the signal for fresh demands, and it was plainly time to resist, if they were not to be robbed of everything. Livingstone's followers adroitly succeeded, in their turn, in surrounding the chief and his councillors, and a deadlock ensued, the leaders of both sides sitting glaring at each other. "I then sat silent for some time", Livingstone records. "It was rather trying for me, because I knew that the Chiboque would aim at the white man first; but I was careful not to appear flurried, and, having four barrels ready for instant action, looked quietly at the savage scene around." In the end, his moral ascendancy was established, and, on offering the further gift of an ox, his party were promised some food. When it came, it turned out to be a very small basket of meal and two or three pounds of the flesh of the ox they had themselves given. "It was impossible to avoid a laugh at the coolness of the generous creatures."

Other travellers have been in situations as unpleasant, and behaved with just the same mild firmness. What distinguishes Livingstone is that he goes on to consider the reason for the hostility he has met with, and to account for it so clearly as to make it sound fully justifiable. "We were taken", he says, "for interlopers trying to cheat the revenue of the tribe." The root of the trouble was, as usual, the slave trade. It was in the nature of the business that the traders had to curry favour with the chiefs whose country they passed through : otherwise the chiefs might offer a refuge to any of their slaves who wished to run away. The traders therefore paid handsomely for the right of passage, and this of course put ideas in the chiefs' heads and sent up the standard price they asked of all travellers. It must be remembered, once again, that the purpose of Livingstone's journey appeared quite incomprehensible to the Chiboque, as to most other Africans. It is not surprising that they were so suspicious, and it is perhaps understandable why their demands should have been extravagant.

In the hope of avoiding further scenes of this kind, Livingstone now altered his course from west, where the people were all known to be familiar with the slave trade, to north, trusting that a route might then be found to the Portuguese settlement of Cassange, which was their goal. To add to his troubles, there were now, for the first and only time on this journey, signs of insubordination among his followers. He was down with an attack of fever at the time in his tent, until finding that his men paid no attention to his orders he decided that stern action must be taken. "I seized a double-barrelled pistol, and darted forth from the domicile, looking, I suppose, so savage as to put them to a precipitate flight." The threat was enough. He had no further trouble of that sort to put up with.

But as the journey dragged on, through this inhospitable country, with no end to it in sight, the men began to talk of going home. Livingstone remonstrated with them, and at last told them that if they insisted on returning he would go on by himself. That brought them round. They renewed their loyalty to him, and their determination to follow him wherever he led, with a touching fidelity.

They were now, if they had known it, drawing near the end of their journey. On 30 March they descended from the high ground they had been traversing into the valley of the Coango. Ill though he was—he had to be supported by his companions as he walked, to prevent him from falling down—Livingstone found its beauty irresistible. Again it recalled the Clyde to him (and he could give it no higher praise), at the point from which Mary Queen of Scots watched the battle of Langside, though the scale of this valley was enormously larger. "Emerging from the gloomy forests of Londa, this magnificent prospect made us all feel as if a weight had been lifted off our eyelids. A cloud was passing across the middle of the valley, from which rolling thunder pealed, while above all was glorious sunlight."

When it came to crossing the river there was another squabble with the owner of the canoes that were necessary. He wanted one price above all for ferrying them over : a man. As the argument was proceeding, a half-caste sergeant of the Portuguese militia turned up, who was in the country looking for bees-wax. He helped them to make an acceptable bargain for the canoes—though not before the people of the owner had opened an inefficient fire on Livingstone's party. When they had crossed the river they were in territory under full Portuguese control, and all difficulties of the kind ceased.

The half-caste sergeant accompanied them on their way and proved a generous host. Livingstone stayed with him a day or two, hoping for a change in the weather, which would disperse the clouds and so enable him to take his observations for determining the position of the Coango. On 10 April they moved on, and after three days' travelling reached Cassange. This was a Portuguese station in the proper sense of the word, and the party was received with the utmost kindness by the first white men they had seen since leaving Kuruman nearly eighteen months before.

Livingstone never forgot the reception the Portuguese gave him in Angola. "Even now, as I copy my journal," he wrote in 1857, "I remember it all with a glow of gratitude." He very quickly discovered the faults of Portuguese rule—only a month later he was writing that "one cannot rely on the most plausible speeches of even Governors. They are excessively corrupt"—and his followers commented as unfavourably as he did on the inadequate cultivation of the rich soil of the country. But nothing could have exceeded the personal kindness he was shown for the whole of the last stage of his journey down to Loanda, and his acknowledgment of it occurs on page after page of the *Missionary Travels*.

He needed it all, for he was now very weak indeed: hardly able to sit on the back of his ox, and too much confused in mind to take his observations or even to remember the names of his companions. In this feeble state, passed on from one hospitable Portuguese station to the next, he tottered on to the west. At last the sea came into sight, and the Makololo expressed their wonder in terms of almost Biblical simplicity. "We marched along with our father," they said, "believing that what the ancients had always told us was true, that the world has no end; but all at once the world said to us, 'I am finished; there is no more of me!'"

They arrived at Loanda on 31 May, the whole party in a state of apprehension. The Makololo were frightened that they would be kidnapped and sold as slaves. All Livingstone's repeated assurances could not allay their fears. As for Livingstone himself, he could not help wondering, in his feverish condition, what he was going to find when he got there. He had been told there was one Englishman in Loanda, to whom he would naturally feel obliged to make his way. What sort of man would he be? The answer was quick, and infinitely reassuring. He was Edmund Gabriel, the British Commissioner for the suppression of the slave trade, and immediately Livingstone arrived, seeing how ill he was, he put him to bed.

In fact, he was a much sicker man than he, or any one else, realised. He intended to make no more than a short stay in Loanda. In the end he was there nearly four months, chiefly because he was so weak, and had become so emaciated, that he was absolutely obliged to recuperate before he could think of travelling. He had the opportunity of going straight back to England. While he was at Loanda, several cruisers of the British naval squadron for the suppression of the slave trade called at the port and offered to take him to St. Helena or any other place from which he could get a passage home. The offer must have been sorely tempting, especially since, to his great disappointment, he had found not a single letter waiting for him at Loanda, and had therefore no idea how things were going with his family. But he had said, before he set out from Linyanti, that he would see his Makololo safely back to their own country. And, apart from that consideration, to return home now would be to leave his work unfinished. His journey from Linyanti to the west coast had proved that it would be difficult to establish any remunerative trade that way. The route to the east coast, down the Zambesi, had still to be tried. For both these compelling reasons, therefore, he refused all the friendly offers that were made to him and bent his mind to preparing for the return journey overland.

All through his long illness at Loanda the Portuguese continued their kindness to him. The Bishop, who was Acting Governor of Angola at the time, was particularly attentive, and Livingstone paid an unstinted tribute, not only to his personal kindness but to the excellence of his work for the people of his diocese. On the Bishop's initiative the government of the province voted a present for Sekeletu, which Livingstone was asked to convey to him, and the merchants of Loanda sent specimens of their wares, together with two donkeys, animals that were said to be immune to the bite of the tsetse-fly. The whole party was re-equipped. Livingstone made a present to each of his men, which included a musket, and he himself had a new tent, made for him by the sailors of H.M.S. *Philomel*. At last, on 20 September, they were able to leave. Gabriel accompanied them for the first thirty miles of their journey, and after they parted he and Livingstone began a long correspondence, of which the letters from Livingstone's side are now in the British Museum. On all his travels, Livingstone never found a kinder friend.

Their route on the return journey was not exactly the same as the one they had previously taken. It included a digression to Massangano, through the prosperous coffee-growing country of Cazengo, and a detour by Pungo Andongo, a Portuguese fort placed in the midst of a group of strange column-like rocks, some three hundred feet high. While he was staying there, Livingstone heard that the papers, maps, and journal he had dispatched home from Loanda had been lost in the shipwreck of the mailboat. At once he sat down to rewrite them. After some days' work on them he felt able to set forward, on New Year's Day, 1855. At Cassange, the last Portuguese outpost, he stopped again for some time, to complete his tedious task. Here, too, he received a bundle of copies of *The Times,* sent up from Loanda, from which he learnt of the outbreak of the Crimean War, and the story of the campaigns down to the Charge of the Light Brigade. He heard no more of it until he reached Tete in March 1856.

In their passage through the country of the Chiboque, the party met the same hostility as before, but it was mitigated by the superior strength they now enjoyed. Though Livingstone was extremely reluctant to shed blood, and in fact had never yet done so, he was not in any sense a pacifist. There is, as we have seen, no evidence that he did anything to arm Sechele's people; but he did not disapprove of allowing Africans to buy firearms. His attitude to the matter was entirely realistic, a typical piece of clear thinking, uninfluenced by false sentiment. The only danger he would admit from the dissemination of firearms among Africans was that it sometimes encouraged a weak tribe to make war on a more powerful one, if it thought it enjoyed a superiority of weapons. Otherwise, "the universal effect of the diffusion of the more potent instruments of warfare in Africa is the same as among ourselves. Firearms render wars less frequent and less bloody. It is indeed exceedingly rare to hear of two tribes having guns going to war with each other." So, among the Chiboque, one of the chiefs who had been most exigent on their way out now changed his tune. Here is Livingstone's dry comment, in a letter to his wife: "The alteration in this gentleman's conduct—the Peace Society would not credit it—is attributable solely to my people possessing guns. When we passed before we were defenceless." [1]

[1] Livingstone's views on pacifism are set out in an interesting letter he wrote to Joseph Sturge in 1858, printed in *Some Letters from Livingstone,* ed. Chamberlin (1940), 268–70.

All the same, they did not get through this troublesome country without any difficulty. For one thing, on 19 April the ordinary intermittent fever, from which Livingstone had again been suffering, turned to a severe attack of rheumatic fever, induced by sleeping on "oblong mounds, somewhat like graves in a country churchyard", raised up from waterlogged ground. This illness detained him over three weeks, and while he was still sick his men became involved in a quarrel with the headman of the village they were staying in. The headman was struck, and put forward an instant demand for compensation for the blow. He rejected what was offered as inadequate, and shooting began. Livingstone thereupon staggered up, bearing a six-barrelled revolver, and was lucky enough to encounter the headman, who at once began to climb down. After a good deal of discussion, the party was allowed to go on its way, but only when Livingstone had shown that he himself was not afraid of the Chiboque by turning his back upon them and riding off on his slow ox. "I do not mention this little skirmish as a very frightful affair", he blandly remarks; going on to observe that these Chiboque and their neighbours were great cowards, except in the moment of success, and not to be compared in point of courage with the Kaffirs of the Cape.

Their journey was painfully slow : they were not usually making more than seven miles a day at this time, and they could reckon only on ten travelling days in the month, allowing for sickness and the interminable delays they were subjected to. As they made their way over the hills towards the Kasai, they took a new route. This was partly in the hope that they might be able to visit the great chief Matiamvo, who lived far away to the north-east. But in the end that idea had to be abandoned, from shortage of goods and from fear that once they had reached the chief it might be difficult to get away from him.

It was after crossing the Kasai and climbing up to Lake Dilolo that Livingstone came to apprehend the structure of the interior of Central Africa. He had already found that this was the watershed between the Kasai, which falls into the Congo and so into the Atlantic, and the Zambesi, flowing out into the Indian Ocean. What he now realised was that this watershed was itself a kind of trough between the mountains of Angola to the west and those that were reported to exist much farther to the east. Later on he learnt that Sir Roderick Murchison had, quite independently, propounded the same idea in an address to the Royal Geographical Society in 1852.

They were now back in friendly country again, and the chiefs who had received them kindly before, like Katema and Shinte, redoubled their welcome now. It was the same all through the Barotse country. At Libonta they "were received with demonstrations of joy such as I had never witnessed before". Livingstone's companions had the pleasure of showing off the finery they had acquired at Loanda and strutting about like the soldiers they had seen there, calling themselves his "braves". But very little of their trading goods remained, after the necessary expenditure of the journey, and "we returned to the Makololo as poor as when we set out". That did not, however, lessen the esteem in which Livingstone was held; his men merely began collecting ivory at once, for use on a second journey to Loanda.

At Sesheke Livingstone at last got some news from the outside world, from a package of letters and goods that had been sent up to him by Moffat and had remained, in a hut constructed expressly for them on an island in the middle of the Zambesi, for about a year. "I found the news was very old", he remarked wryly, "and had lost much of its interest by keeping, but there were some good eatables from Mrs. Moffat." A few days later he went on to Linyanti, where everything that he had left behind when he started, nearly two years earlier, was still perfectly safe.

The Makololo received the returning party with the utmost pleasure. Sekeletu was delighted with his presents, and on Sunday when he "made his appearance at church in his uniform, it excited more attention than the sermon". Livingstone was gratified to find that volunteers were forthcoming to accompany him to the east coast, and that Sekeletu at once decided to send a fresh party to Loanda to develop the trade that had thus, with so much difficulty, been begun. He was less pleased at discovering that while he was away on his journey Sekeletu and his people had undertaken two expeditions for the purpose of stealing cattle. He remonstrated with the chief, but there was no more he could do.

For the eastward journey he was now contemplating, he had the choice of two main routes. An East Coast Arab who was at Linyanti at the time advised him to make his way across country to the north-east, and so to Zanzibar. He represented the African chiefs whose territory lay on the way as friendly and said the journey would be an easy one. But Livingstone believed that the real need was to open up communication with Central Africa by water, rather than overland; and the Makololo, on their part, advised him strongly to follow the line of the Zambesi. Their opinion was entitled to some respect, for they had formerly lived much lower down the river themselves. The only serious obstacle they admitted was the great falls and the succeeding chain of rapids, a short distance away; but though they would be an impediment to water-borne trade, they need not seriously hinder Livingstone now. Having decided in favour of the Zambesi route, it remained for him to determine on which side of the river he should march. Again he received conflicting advice; but he decided in favour of the north side on the basis of Bowdich's map of 1824, which placed Tete, the westernmost of the Portuguese stations, on that side of the river.

Once again, Sekeletu proved a generous host. He prevailed on Livingstone to wait until the first rains before starting, and when the expedition did set off, on 3 November, he insisted, as before, on accompanying it on the first stages of its way. He supplied twelve oxen and enough beads to buy a canoe when they rejoined the Zambesi below the falls. "He likewise presented abundance of fresh butter and honey, and did everything in his power to make me comfortable for the journey. I was entirely dependent on his generosity."

It was not Livingstone's intention to follow the Zambesi at first, but to strike away to the north-east and to pick it up again a good deal lower down, below the long series of rapids, of which the Makololo had told him. But he felt he must see the great falls for himself, as they lay only a short distance out of his way. The Makololo called them "Mosioatunya", meaning "smoke sounds there", an allusion to the great columns of vapour that rose from the roaring falls. Livingstone gives a fine and elaborate account of them—it is the one set-piece in the 700 pages of the *Missionary Travels*. They moved him to do two things he had never done before in Africa. Having planted a little garden on an island on the very lip of the falls, he cut his initials and the year "1855" on one of its trees; and he christened the falls with the name of his Queen, which they have always borne since.

By the end of November they had climbed up to the old home of the Makololo, from which they had been driven by the Matebele in Sebituane's time. It is the country round Kalomo, now traversed by the railway from Lusaka before it drops down to cross the Zambesi at the Victoria Falls. Livingstone's people spoke of it as "a perfect paradise", and he was much of their opinion. It had a dry soil, yet plenty of water. The temperature was moderate. It afforded good pasture for cattle, and abundant game. Great trees grew in it. Here was something nearer to what he was searching for : a healthy site for a mission-station in the heart of Central Africa. He was immensely cheered by the discovery : "The enjoyment of good health in fine open scenery had an exhilarating effect on my spirits."

They now passed through the country of the Batoka,

with some of whom the Makololo were on bad terms. Their reception of the visitors was perfectly friendly, but Livingstone was distressed at their low degree of civilisation. He was making for the Kafue river, intending to travel down its valley to meet the Zambesi, of which it was a tributary. At the point where they struck the Kafue they were most hospitably received by a chief named Semalembue, who gave them an enormous present of food. Livingstone apologised for having little to give him in return, but Semalembue replied "that he knew there were no goods in the country from which I had come, and, in professing great joy at the words of peace I spoke, he said, 'Now I shall cultivate largely, in the hope of eating and sleeping in peace". "It is noticeable", Livingstone adds, "that all whom we have yet met eagerly caught up the idea of living in peace as the probable effect of the gospel." Day after day, as they travelled on, he remarked on the beauty of the country and its profusion of game. Close to the confluence of the Kafue and the Zambesi they stood on high ground, surveying a great plain to the north, richer in great wild animals than anywhere else Livingstone had seen. "Hundreds of buffaloes and zebras grazed on the open spaces, and there stood lordly elephants feeding majestically, nothing moving apparently but the proboscis. I wished that I had been able to take a photograph of a scene, so seldom beheld, and which is destined, as guns increase, to pass away from earth." Though Livingstone had lived much with big-game hunters in Bechuanaland, and counted some of them among his friends, he never approved of their sport. To the end of his life he remained profoundly interested in the animals of Africa, and he devoted many pages of his journals to describing them. But he thought of them always as living creatures. It might be justifiable to kill them for a practical purpose—for food, for their feathers or their hides; but if "great numbers of animals are wounded and allowed to perish miserably, or are killed on the spot and left to be preyed on by vultures and hyænas, and all for the sole

66

purpose of making a 'bag', then I take it to be evident that such sportsmen are pretty far gone in the hunting form of insanity".

An unwonted, almost idyllic tone runs through the whole of Livingstone's account of this part of his journey. It ceases, abruptly, on 14 January 1856. They had reached the Loangwe, one of the largest of the Zambesi's tributaries. The river being in flood, it was about half a mile broad, and they needed to be ferried across it. But the people's behaviour was so suspicious that the party thought they would be attacked on their passage over. Livingstone shared their premonitions. His quiet reflection at this point shows the unchanging serenity that carried him through all such dangers : "I felt some turmoil of spirit in the evening, at the prospect of having all my efforts for the welfare of this great region and its teeming population, knocked on the head by savages tomorrow, who might be said to 'know not what they do'. . . . But I read that Jesus said, 'All power is given unto me in heaven and on earth : go ye, therefore, and teach all nations . . . and lo, *I am with you alway, even unto the end of the world*'. I took this as His word of honour, and then went out to take observations for latitude and longitude, which, I think, were very successful." In the end they all got across safely, and Livingstone reflects that the people were perhaps only taking natural precautions, "for they have reason to be distrustful of the whites".

The place they had now reached had once been a Portuguese station named Zumbo. There were the ruins of a church and a fort and eight or ten houses, all built of stone. Though the settlement was now wholly deserted, they at least knew they were approaching the lower part of the river, under effective Portuguese domination. A little farther on they learnt that Bowdich's map had misinformed them : Tete was on the right bank of the Zambesi. But they crossed the river in safety, and after a further very weary march of five weeks they approached

the town. They stopped for the night of 2 March eight
miles off, and Livingstone sent forward to the Commandant letters of introduction he had been given by the
Bishop and other Portuguese in Angola. At two o'clock in
the morning they were woken up by the arrival of a small
detachment of Portuguese troops, sent out with a breakfast for Livingstone. "Though I had just been too tired
to sleep, all my fatigue vanished. It was the most refreshing breakfast I ever partook of, and I walked the last
eight miles without the least feeling of weariness. . . . The
pleasure experienced in partaking of that breakfast was
only equalled by the enjoyment of Mr. Gabriel's bed on
my arrival at Loanda. It was also enhanced by the news
that Sebastopol had fallen, and the war was finished."

As in Angola, so at Tete and throughout Portuguese
East Africa, Livingstone met with unbounded hospitality.
The Commandant, Major Sicard, pressed him to stay at
Tete until the following month, to avoid the most unhealthy season in the delta. He looked after the Makololo
with the same care. The delay gave Livingstone an opportunity to form an estimate of the condition and prospects
of this part of the country. Potentially it was rich, not
only in soil but in minerals : gold and iron were worked,
though on a very small scale, and nine seams of coal
were known. But the actual state of Tete and its surrounding countryside was miserable. The settlement itself
had been much damaged (except for the fort, which was
in good repair), and its trade entirely dislocated, by a
rebellion, and though Major Sicard was doing what he
could to re-establish confidence in the Africans, Tete was
still a dilapidated and spiritless place. After a stay of
seven weeks there, Livingstone moved on down the Zambesi to Sena, the next Portuguese station, which he found
"ten times worse". The Portuguese at Sena were barely
able to defend themselves against the neighbouring tribes:
even their fort was grass-grown. A hopeless decay seemed
to have settled upon the whole colony. Its budget went
unbalanced, the pay of its officers was years behind, and

they kept alive only by private trading on their own account. And yet, for all his contempt for the administration of the Portuguese, he continually acknowledges his indebtedness to them. "I ought to speak well for ever of Portuguese hospitality. I have noted each little act of civility received, because somehow or other we have come to hold the Portuguese character in rather a low estimation. . . . If my specification of their kindnesses will tend to engender a more respectful feeling to the nation, I shall consider myself well rewarded."

The last stage of his journey now began, from Sena to Quilimane in the Zambesi delta. A little way down, the river receives the last of its great tributaries : the Shire, which flows in beneath Mount Morambala. Livingstone was most anxious to climb the mountain, feeling that it might provide the site for a station of the kind he was searching for, but his hosts refused to let him, as the people were unfriendly. Even in passing, however, he could see that Morambala was only the last of a chain of mountains—the Shire Highlands, which he determined to revisit as soon as he could. Passing by with reluctance, he went straight on down the river to Quilimane, where he arrived on 20 May. He had crossed the continent from Loanda in exactly twenty months.

The joy that he felt on arriving at his destination was ruined by the news that two officers and five seamen of H.M.S. *Dart* had been drowned in crossing the bar of the river on their way to try to get news of him. He was much upset, too, by a letter he received there from the London Missionary Society, in which handsome congratulation on his work was accompanied by the statement that the Directors "were restricted in their power of aiding plans connected only remotely with the spread of the Gospel, and that the financial circumstances of the Society were not such as to afford any ground of hope that it would be in a position, within any definite period, to enter upon untried, remote, and difficult fields of labour". The words are important, in view of the subsequent relations between

Livingstone and the Society. They were not happily chosen. Livingstone was certainly a little touchy—and he became more so as he grew older. But to speak of his plans as "connected only remotely with the spread of the Gospel" must have looked to him like a calculated slight, a rejection of all the work he had been trying to do, in the face of untold difficulty and suffering, for the past four years.

He had to wait six weeks at Quilimane for the arrival of another British ship. He employed the time, as usual, in observing the country round him, above all in learning what he could about the Zambesi delta; for it was a necessary condition of the development of the interior that a way should be found into the river, safer and more convenient than that by Quilimane. At last, early in July, H.M.S. *Frolic* arrived and took him on board, in a frightful sea, together with the leader of his African companions, Sekwebu, who had begged to be allowed to go on with him to England. Livingstone noted that he found it difficult at first to express himself in English on board ship : it was so long since he had spoken his own language that he was constantly casting about for words that would not come. The *Frolic* took them to Mauritius, where poor Sekwebu became insane, jumped overboard, and was drowned. Again Livingstone was hospitably detained, by the British Governor, General Hay, who insisted that he must recuperate in his genial island before returning home. He set sail in the autumn, once more escaped death narrowly in an accident to his P. & O. liner in the Bay of Tunis, and arrived in England on 9 November 1856.

Chapter Five

First Visit Home
(1856–1858)

SIX months had elapsed between Livingstone's arrival at Quilimane and his return to England. The news of his success preceded him, and when he reached London he was received with the warmest acclamation. On 15 December a special meeting of the Royal Geographical Society was held, at which he was formally presented with the Society's gold medal—the highest honour it had to bestow, awarded to him during his absence in Africa in 1855. The medal was presented by Sir Roderick Murchison, the President of the Society, who was already, as we have seen, interested in the same geographical problems as Livingstone. It was the beginning of a cordial friendship, which meant much to them both and ended only with Murchison's death in 1871.

In replying to Murchison's congratulatory address, Livingstone began—as he usually did in the months of speechifying that he was now entering upon—by apologising for his shortcomings, on the ground that his English was still rusty. There is little sign of this in the reports of his speeches or the descriptions of them left by his hearers; and none at all in the written narrative of his travels. But it was not a merely conventional, humbugging piece of self-dispraisal. He was a genuinely nervous public speaker, and remained so all his life. And modesty, with him, was entirely sincere. "As a Christian missionary," he said in his speech on this occasion, "I only did my duty in attempting to open up part of southern intertropical Africa to the sympathy of Christendom. . . . Some of the members of your Society, Colonel Steele, Captain Vardon, and Mr. Oswell for instance, could, either of them, have effected all I have done." But he made it immediately clear, in this very first speech, that his achievement was only a prelude to further work in Africa that he intended to undertake. "A man may boast when he is putting off his armour," he remarked, "but I am just putting mine on."

The next day his own London Missionary Society held a reception in his honour, presided over by Lord Shaftesbury, and gave him a dinner. In spite of the unfortunately worded letter he had received from the Society at Quilimane, Livingstone's public acknowledgment of the support afforded to him by the Directors was generous now. There was nothing to show, as yet, that he was considering the possibility of leaving their service, though he had already, in fact, made up his mind to do so.

One task lay directly ahead of him. At Murchison's suggestion, he agreed with John Murray to write an account of his travels. In doing so he seems to have been fortified by two beliefs : that the work would be quick and easy, and that it would save him from having to make a great many further public appearances. He soon found that both these notions were mistaken. "Those who have never carried a book through the press", he wrote in retrospect, "can form no idea of the amount of toil it involves. The process has increased my respect for authors and authoresses a hundred-fold." It is no wonder that he found the work so hard. Not only was he unaccustomed to it, labouring to express himself in words, which had never come very fluently to him : he was also writing against time. He had told his Makololo, when he left them behind at Tete in April 1856, that he would return to Africa a year later and lead them back to their own country; and when he began writing his book, in the second half of January 1857, he seems still to have believed, quite seriously, that this time-table could be kept.

It was, of course, impossible. But it is, none the less, extraordinary to find that the *Missionary Travels and Researches in South Africa,* a book of 300,000 words, was put together in little more than six months. While he was writing it, Livingstone stayed in London with friends, or in suburban lodgings, his family around him—as absorbed and undistracted by the children as he had been with his Latin grammar in the cotton-mill, or with his Bible and his astronomical observations in the middle of Africa. The book was published in November 1857 at a guinea, and at once had a great success. The first edition of 12,000 copies was over-subscribed before it was published.

This success was thoroughly well deserved. The book is a clear and palpably honest account of one of the historic journeys of the world : satisfying in its fullness and the accuracy of its observation. The narrative, though there is a Victorian amplitude about it, is not prolix : it is often taut, sometimes exciting, and humorous, too, in an astringent Scots manner. For all the success it won at the time and the permanent place it retains in the library of exploration, it may be questioned whether the literary merit of the book has ever been recognised quite as it deserves. Livingstone's biographers have usually been a little apologetic about it. In the official *Life,* speaking of this book, Blaikie thinks it right to explain that "he had no time to plan, to shape, to organise; the architectural talent could not be brought into play". But "the architectural talent" would surely have been misplaced here. The book is a narrative, and Livingstone's simple instinct was perfectly sound, in leaving it as plain narrative and nothing more. The result is to give the reader an overpowering sense of the absolute truth of the story : that is why, in its workaday English, it is so life-like and often so moving. Even the occasional *longueurs* are in place, with unintended effect, serving to remind us of the tedium from which Livingstone himself suffered so much in travelling. Altogether, the *Missionary Travels* may

73

fairly be claimed as one of the great books that we owe to unprofessional writers.

If Livingstone really supposed that by printing an account of his work he would escape further demands for his appearance in public, he was entirely mistaken. As long as he could plead that he was engaged on his book, he was safe from such persecution. But as the writing drew to a close, he found himself forced to accept some at least of the invitations that showered in upon him. In August 1857 he was a principal speaker at the meeting of the British Association in Dublin. "Dr. Livingstone's lecture I should like everybody to have heard", wrote one of his audience on that occasion. "People say it was signally lacking in arrangement, but I have no nose for logic; I thought one just mounted his ox and went on behind him." [1] He then went on to address the Manchester Chamber of Commerce, chiefly on the economic resources of the region he had discovered. He had news, indeed, of special interest for Manchester : for he had found cotton under cultivation on the Zambesi. His next move was to Scotland. The reception he met with in Glasgow summarises very well the breadth of his appeal to his countrymen. He was honoured by the corporation, by the university, by the physicians and surgeons, by the United Presbyterians, and by the cotton-workers, who recognised in him the greatest man who had ever emerged from their ranks. Two thousand pounds was subscribed for a testimonial in his honour. His own people had a chance of showing their pride in him, at Hamilton and Blantyre. Then, as the autumn went on, he resumed his more trying formal appearances before companies of strangers in Edinburgh, in the great industrial towns of northern England, and finally at Oxford and Cambridge.

Meanwhile he was considering his plans for the future. The tactless letter he had received at Quilimane from the

---

[1] *Memories of Old Friends: being Extracts from the Journals and Letters of Caroline Fox,* ed. H. N. Pym (2nd ed., 1882), ii. 256.

London Missionary Society had determined him to leave the Society's service. He decided on this course before ever he reached home; and, although the Directors made it clear that no offence whatever had been intended and that they valued his services very highly, he did not change his mind. He recognised that it was better for the Society and for him that they should separate. It must be remembered that the Directors had no absolute powers; and if they aided work that was as much scientific as religious they would run the risk of severe criticism from the main body of subscribers, to whom they were answerable. On his side Livingstone could not consider sacrificing his freedom to pursue his own unique work in the way he thought best. So, without overt unkindness, the Society and he parted company.

At the British Association meeting in Dublin a plan was set on foot for inviting the government to assist his work. The approach was made and met with an immediately favourable response. Palmerston was Prime Minister at the time, and he had long taken the closest interest in the suppression of the slave trade. It had been one of the principal elements in his foreign policy. "During the many years that I was at the Foreign Office", he wrote in 1864, "there was no subject that more constantly or more intensely occupied my thoughts, or constituted the aim of my labours. . . . The achievement which I look back to with the greatest and purest pleasure was the forcing the Brazilians to give up their slave trade." Clarendon, who was now Foreign Secretary, was equally determined in the matter. Livingstone therefore found the two most important members of the government ready, indeed eager, to assist him.

His ideas were now entirely directed towards revisiting the lower valley of the Zambesi. It seemed, from what he had observed of it, to offer an almost perfect field for the policy he now wished to develop. The country was potentially fertile and rich in minerals : an attractive field, then, for European commercial enterprise, which could,

75

imperceptibly, destroy the slave trade through offering the Africans bigger returns for less risk. The great river appeared navigable throughout its lower course, except at one place—the Kebrabasa Rapids above Tete. Livingstone had not seen them himself, for he was marching south of the river at that point, but he did not consider that they could be a serious obstacle. Surely a steamer of adequate power could sail up them, at least in the flood season? The Zambesi, moreover, had another important merit, in the highlands that lay close to it. This was the clear advantage it possessed over all the other great African rivers. There need be none of the dreadful loss of life that had attended the opening-up of the Niger; for here there were innumerable sites for healthy stations, to which Europeans could retire to recuperate from sickness. It is not surprising that Livingstone should have chosen the Zambesi as his next field of work.

An elaborate plan, on a big scale, was drawn up for him at the Admiralty. When Livingstone, with a wise instinct, rejected it, Clarendon said to him : "Just come here and tell me what you want, and I will give it you." An invitation in this form exactly suited Livingstone's temperament. He had never tried to manage a large company of white men, nor had he ever worked with a government department. What he wanted was something much simpler, more modest and more easily directed: Clarendon's invitation gave him his opportunity to get it. Five thousand pounds was forthcoming from the Treasury—a sum of almost inconceivable magnitude to Livingstone, accustomed to subsisting on the London Missionary Society's £100 a year. By January 1858 he had completed the detailed plan of his operations and submitted it to Clarendon, together with the names of five of the six Europeans he proposed to take with him. Neither the Foreign Office nor the Admiralty made the least demur.

Clarendon's official instructions to Livingstone, as commander of the Expedition, were based entirely on his own scheme. In view of what followed, it is important to remember that the government merely acted, in effect, at Livingstone's behest. It did not attempt to force him to do anything against his will.

The serene confidence that Palmerston and Clarendon displayed in Livingstone is very remarkable. They were both men of the world, well-seasoned politicians; neither of them showed the smallest strain of the impractical idealist. Yet, with this man they were trusting so implicitly, they had very little to go upon except the record of his journeys and the impression he made on them in personal intercourse. There is the heart of it all—something that is beyond our recovery now. Livingstone owed his power over other men not to his charm of manner but to the force and earnestness of his purpose. He was never a fluent speaker. He carried conviction, especially with such hard-headed men as these politicians, by mastery of his subject and single-minded determination. He had come back to England possessed by the importance of opening up the Zambesi valley. His exposition of his policy was impressive and cogent : he so clearly knew what he was talking about. Neither Palmerston nor Clarendon was particularly susceptible to the missionary aspect of his work; but they supported him just as strongly as the missionaries, on quite different grounds.

It might be suggested that in doing so they were merely humouring public opinion. Livingstone became, indeed, a national figure in 1857, and the government won popularity by assisting him. But the policy brought difficulties with it, for which Palmerston and Clarendon were prepared from the start. If the Expedition was to succeed, the co-operation of the Portuguese was essential, for the Zambesi ran through their territory, and if they were inclined to be touchy or obstructive they would be able to do much to ruin Livingstone's work from the outset. Now touchiness and obstruction were well-established characteristics of Portuguese policy : particularly in colonial matters, and most especially where the slave trade was concerned. At this moment the government in Lisbon was attacking the slave trade with some vigour. In 1856 it had passed laws emancipating a large number of slaves in the colonies; it had prohibited the export of Africans from Portuguese territory under the French "Free Labour Emigration System"—which was the slave trade in an ingeniously disguised form; and in this very summer of 1857 it had dismissed the Governor-General of Mozambique and appointed his successor "for the express purpose of enforcing that prohibition and of otherwise suppressing the slave trade". But it was one thing for the Portuguese government to pursue this policy on its own initiative : another for it to give facilities—let alone a welcome—to a British expedition, which might pry into corners better kept dark.

Clarendon's diplomatic preparations, however, were thorough and successful. The Lisbon government promised to afford the Expedition all the support it could and issued immediate instructions in this sense to its principal officers in East Africa. Difficulty arose on one point alone. Clarendon wished to create for Livingstone the appointment of British consul at Quilimane, Sena, and Tete, hoping that this would secure him "more respect and attention from the Portuguese authorities". But the Portuguese government refused its consent to this proposal, on the ground that though Quilimane, in the delta, was open to foreign trade, Sena and Tete were not. Clarendon had necessarily to give way, and in the end Livingstone was accredited as consul for Quilimane alone, though with a general roving commission to the Africans of the interior beyond Portuguese jurisdiction. At this stage, it might seem hardly more than a matter of words; but it was an unpleasant omen for the success of the plan to open up the Zambesi to European commerce.

Though Livingstone was thus leaving the London Missionary Society to serve under the government, that did not mean that he had lost his old belief in missions. Throughout his three months of "public spouting" he had steadfastly urged upon his audiences the importance of missionary work. The climax of it all came at the end of the series, at Cambridge. He had been kindly welcomed at Oxford, though not more kindly than elsewhere. But at Cambridge his reception was memorable. He found new friends, in Whewell, the Master of Trinity, and especially in Adam Sedgwick, Professor of Geology, who became one of his warmest admirers. He spoke in the Senate House on the morning of 4 December 1857. We have an almost verbatim report of the speech. The body of it was no more than a summary of the *Missionary Travels*—the same speech, no doubt, as he had made twenty times before in the course of that autumn. But as he approached the end he seemed to draw inspiration from his audience, and he made a direct appeal to them for missionaries to go to Africa. "The sort of men who are wanted for missionaries", he said, "are such as I see before me—men of education, standing, enterprise, zeal, and piety. It is a mistake to suppose that *any one,* as long as he is pious, will do for this office. Pioneers in everything should be the ablest and best qualified men." He must have felt the response to his words. A minute or two later he reached the end of his speech. There was a pause; and then, his voice rising to a shout, he proclaimed his final message to them : "I beg to direct your attention to Africa. I know that in a few years I shall be cut off in that country, which is now open; do not let it be shut again ! I go back to Africa to try to make an open path for commerce and Christianity; do you carry out the work which I have begun. I LEAVE IT WITH YOU !" Sedgwick, who had been present on all the great occasions in that place from the time of the Napoleonic wars, said that none had ever aroused more intense excitement.

The enthusiasm that Livingstone stirred up that morning at Cambridge had a lasting and notable consequence, in the foundation of a new missionary body, known at first as the Oxford, Cambridge, Dublin, and Durham Mission, and later as the Universities Mission to Central

Africa. It is characteristic of Livingstone that the one mission that derived its origin from him sprang from a denomination widely different from his own. The U.M.C.A. was a strictly Anglican body from the outset. But Livingstone was the very opposite of a sectarian. He thought an episcopal form of organisation was the best adapted for missionary work, and the practical consideration weighed most with him. The founders of the new mission followed his teaching very closely. Its objects were to be not only evangelisation but "the advancement of science and the useful arts" and constant combat with the slave trade. The mission owed its foundation, and the principles of its work, to Livingstone. He regarded it from the start with a passionate and jealous affection, expecting from it the same exalted standards of performance as he imposed on himself.

Though he had now severed his connection with the London Missionary Society, it continued to be influenced by him. The account he had given of the Makololo interested the Society in the idea of sending a mission to them. It was also considering the establishment of one with the Matebele, to whom Robert Moffat was paying his fourth visit at this time. The plans went forward slowly at the Society's headquarters, and Livingstone, who would not be in England much longer, determined to speed them up in a drastic and masterful way. His wife's brother, John Smith Moffat, was in training as a missionary and willing to go out into this field. He was also anxious to get married. Livingstone enabled him to do both. "My dear brother," he wrote abruptly on 6 February 1858, "if you will go to the Makololo country and conscientiously do your duty as a missionary to them or to the Matebele, I shall most gladly pay you £500 down on Monday next and give you my waggon at Capetown. . . . This, with the hire of another, would secure your passage up the country comfortably, and then I engage to pay you £150 per annum afterwards so long as I live. This would come out of my salary. . . . Now don't reject this because it is the proposal of one man. I meant to do good with my increased means." The offer was gratefully accepted. Moffat chose to work with the Matebele, as his father had done; and in due course the London Missionary Society decided to establish its station among the Makololo, sending out a party in 1858, which made its way up from the Cape by Livingstone's old route to Linyanti.

The early months of 1858 passed in intensive preparations for the Expedition. A steamer was built, specially designed for it by Macgregor Laird of Birkenhead, who had had twenty years' experience of the use of steamships on the Niger. The members of the Expedition were briefed, equipment and provisions ordered—on a scale far beyond Livingstone's previous experience. On 13 February he was summoned to an interview with the Queen. To Africans who questioned him about her, it had always seemed strange that he had never seen her: now he would be able to describe her to them from his personal knowledge. On the same day he was the guest of honour at a large banquet. The long series of flattering speeches made, by Murchison and the Duke of Argyll, by Bishop Wilberforce and Richard Owen, must have irked him. But the Duke observed that as Ulva, from which the Livingstones sprang, was close to Iona, so David Livingstone's work in Africa might come to be compared to that of Columba in Europe. It was a happy inspiration, and it may be said to have been largely fulfilled.

Inevitably the preparations took longer than had been expected. Livingstone was determined to be off in the middle of February. But he was demanding the impossible, and it was not until the beginning of March that all was ready. The little steamer, which had run her trials in the Mersey, was christened the *Ma Robert* (from the Africans' name for Mrs. Livingstone) and stowed on board the S.S. *Pearl* for the passage out. The members of the Expedition assembled at Liverpool, and on 10 March they sailed.

Chapter Six

Chapter Six

The Zambesi Expedition
(1858—1864)

THE Zambesi Expedition was an utterly different
affair from the great journey of 1852–1856. On that
journey Livingstone had been the servant of a missionary
society, and his resources had been meagre; he had taken
with him a minimum of equipment—much less than a
minimum from the point of view of his health; his only
companions had been Africans. He sailed for the Zambesi
in 1858, on the other hand, as an accredited agent of the
British government, with a steamship and other equipment that had cost £5,000, and a salary five times what
the London Missionary Society had paid him. Most important of all for the fate of the Expedition, he set out
with six white men under his command. All these changes
were designed to strengthen Livingstone's position. On
paper, the Zambesi Expedition should have been able to
accomplish far more than he had achieved single-handed.
But, for one reason and another, most of these advantages
turned out in the end to be less valuable than they seemed,
or even to be actual drawbacks. The Expedition was,
comparatively speaking, a failure, and some of the causes
of its failure were there before ever it reached Africa.

In the choice of men, as in everything else, the British
government had given Livingstone a free hand. He had
no one forced upon him against his will. But it was a
necessary consequence of his earlier life, his long absence
from England, that he knew very few people indeed who
might be considered possible colleagues. His younger

brother Charles, as it happened, was at home in 1857, and he determined to take him to fill the post of general assistant and what he quaintly called "moral agent". As naval officer to the Expedition, Livingstone selected Commander Norman Bedingfeld. He had been in command of H.M.S. *Pluto* at Loanda when Livingstone arrived there in 1854. The two had formed a favourable opinion of each other then, and on learning of the preparations for the Zambesi Expedition, Bedingfeld volunteered to serve on it.

The other four men were personally quite unknown to Livingstone : he chose them on what seemed good recommendation. As ship's engineer he appointed George Rae, as mining engineer Richard Thornton, who was vouched for by Sir Roderick Murchison. Thomas Baines was selected as "artist and storekeeper". He had been in Africa before, accompanying the British troops as an artist in the Kaffir Wars from 1848 to 1851, and he had just been serving on Gregory's expedition in north-western Australia. Lastly, John Kirk was appointed botanist and medical officer. He was only twenty-five, but he had already made some contributions to botanical knowledge. He was warmly recommended by the Director at Kew and by his professors at Edinburgh University.

There was nothing evidently wrong with any of these appointments. Livingstone might be expected to know his own brother's character—though it should be remembered that they had not met for seventeen years. The other men were all supported by the favourable testimony of good judges. The really unknown factor was Livingstone's capacity to lead and manage them. That was something he had never had to do before. His power of handling Africans was plain enough from the story of his first great journey, but that was no qualification for the very different task of heading an expedition of Europeans.

On the voyage out they called first at Freetown, where they picked up twelve of the Kroomen of that coast, a people renowned for their skill in handling boats. On

21 April they reached the Cape. Livingstone's reception
there was in comic contrast to his experiences on his last
visit in 1852. The Cape government had then looked on
him as a suspicious character, and had done its best to
prevent him from buying arms and ammunition. Now he
found a welcome of embarrassing warmth : the Governor,
Sir George Grey, presented him with a silver box containing 800 guineas, raised by a public subscription in the
colony; the Attorney-General presided at a dinner in
honour of the members of the Expedition. Ten days later
they set off again, on the last stage of their journey, and
on 15 May they made their first attempt to enter the
Zambesi.

Very little was known about the delta of the river, and
it was the first task of the Expedition to secure an accurate
account of it, since the whole plan on which it was based
depended on the possibility of finding an easy route into
the Zambesi from the sea. Quilimane, by which the
Portuguese travelled, was not on a true arm of the
Zambesi at all, though accessible from it by an intricate
system of creeks; and in any case it was a thoroughly unsuitable station for the purpose—it was pestilential and
could be reached from the sea only over a dangerous bar.

The first attempt proved abortive, but the second, up
the Kongone mouth, was successful. It appeared at once,
however, that the river would be too shallow for the
draught of the *Pearl*, and Livingstone decided to disem-
bark the goods from her and send her home, relying on the
Ma Robert for the future. On 26 June she sailed away,
and the members of the Expedition were cut off from all
but very intermittent contact with the outside world.

Even before she left, their harmony had been broken.
Livingstone and Bedingfeld had begun to quarrel. Kirk
was doubtless right in remarking that Bedingfeld was
"tired of the service; he seems to have expected to live the
life of a man-of-war commander and has no idea of being
a subordinate". In truth, there was no job for him to do.
As a senior naval officer he thought himself above the

mere business of looking after the *Ma Robert*. Moreover, it very quickly appeared that she was a thoroughly inefficient vessel, and since Bedingfeld alone had been present at her trials in the Mersey, Livingstone may well have shown that he held him partly responsible for her failure. At all events, after much unpleasantness Bedingfeld resigned and was taken down to Quilimane to await the next passing ship to convey him home. In the subsequent inquiries, the Foreign Office and the Admiralty both upheld Livingstone. It is probable that he was in the right; but the episode gave a disagreeable start to the Expedition, and Kirk noted that Charles Livingstone childishly refused to speak to Bedingfeld and insisted on making "a private quarrel" of it.

As they moved slowly up the river they learnt there had been a resurgence of the rebellion against the Portuguese of which Livingstone had heard in 1856. At Shupanga they found themselves "in the sickening smell, and among the mutilated bodies of the slain", and Kirk was soon busy tending the wounded. Livingstone meanwhile passed on up to Tete, where he was tumultuously welcomed by his old party of Makololo.

It was not until the beginning of November that the whole party was reunited and the next task could be begun. One of the objects of bringing out the *Ma Robert* had been to try the possibility of sailing up the Zambesi, at the flood season of the year, by the power of steam. Livingstone knew that there was the formidable series of the Kebrabasa Rapids some sixty miles upstream from Tete, though he had not seen them in 1856 because he was making a detour to the south of the river at that point. He now paid three visits to them. The first was a brief and inconclusive survey. On the second, he was accompanied only by Kirk and three of the Makololo. "It was as tough a bit of travel as they ever had in Africa", Livingstone remarked. The rapids lay in a gorge, and the only way of getting close enough to examine them was to climb along its side. The rocks were slippery, and so intensely hot that the Africans' feet became blistered; it was impossible to hold on to them for any length of time with the hands. The Makololo implored Livingstone to return, saying they "always thought he had a heart, but now they believed he had none"; and when he refused they seriously supposed he had gone insane. It was understandable : yet this adamant, ruthless determination to go on until the problem was solved was entirely in accordance with his character. Nothing would induce him to turn back, and in the end they all came through alive, the answer to the problem found. As a result of this examination of the rapids, Livingstone had to admit that they were a fatal obstacle to all ordinary traffic up the river, though he reported home to the government that "a steamer of light draught and capable of going 12 or 14 knots an hour would pass up the rapids without difficulty when the river is in full flood in January or February".

Unfortunately, this could be no more than an opinion —and Kirk regarded it as an over-optimistic one : for the *Ma Robert* was much too feeble a craft to be used in a demonstration. From the very first she gave nothing but trouble. It took four hours—from two to six every morning—to get steam up in her, and then she steamed so badly that they called her "the Asthmatic". On a new principle, she had been built of steel plates only a sixtenth of an inch thick, and she quickly began to leak like a colander. Livingstone observed, with studied mildness, in his book on the Expedition that "to build an exploring ship of untried material was a mistake". It is the only mild remark on the subject that is recorded of him. The *Ma Robert* drove him to frenzied indignation, and led him to vilify Laird, the builder, in scandalous terms. "This is a sham of a thing", he wrote to his brother-in-law; "it cannot stem a three-and-a-half knot current and was evidently planned to get another job soon. Macgregor Laird heard Lord Clarendon say to me, 'We shall assist you with all the power of the government', and resolved to play as much money into his own hands as

possible." Nothing that we know of Macgregor Laird—
who steadfastly assisted the exploration of West Africa—
suggests that there was a syllable of truth in Livingstone's
accusations. But his fury can easily be understood; for the
failure of the *Ma Robert* balked the Expedition of much
of its success from the start.

For the moment, all he could do was to write home to
the government, representing the hopeless defects of the
steamer he had and asking for another, more powerful
and better built, to replace her; and to turn away from
the Zambesi to examine the country lying to the north,
which had excited his interest in 1856. The gateway to it
was the River Shire, which joins the Zambesi a little
below Sena. Leaving the other Englishmen behind at
Tete, Livingstone and Kirk set off in the *Ma Robert* on
20 December. Ten days later they were climbing
Mount Morambala, a little way up the Shire on its left
bank. They found it was in reality a large plateau, 4,000
feet high, covered in rich vegetation, its atmosphere "pure
and bracing". At once they seemed to be getting nearer
to finding the site for a healthy station that they were
always searching for. The people of the waterside were
not disposed to be friendly. One of their chiefs, Tingane,
had consistently refused to allow traders from the Portuguese settlements to pass through his territory on slaving
expeditions, and he peremptorily ordered the *Ma Robert*
to stop. But Livingstone landed and explained to him that
his party had no connection with the Portuguese and
nothing to do with slaving. As soon as he found out that
Livingstone was an Englishman, merely prospecting for
cotton in the ordinary way of trade, Tingane became
friendly. Again and again Livingstone notes that the
people of the interior, even though they had never seen
either Portuguese or Englishmen, put them into quite
different categories. "Ah, you must be one of the tribe
that has a heart towards the black men", exclaimed one
fierce chief, who was actually at war with the Portuguese.
At the same time, on his usual principles, Livingstone

added some words to Tingane and his people about the Christian God.

Two hundred miles upstream, they found the course of the river barred, once again, by a series of rapids. Livingstone decided to call them "after one whose name has already a world-wide fame, and whose generous kindness we can never repay": they have been known as the Murchison Cataracts ever since. They were forced to turn back, but as soon as they reached Tete Livingstone and Kirk began to prepare for a journey much farther in the same direction, overland. They started again in March, left the *Ma Robert* at Chibisa, just below the cataracts, and broke away from the river to the east, accompanied by a party of sixteen Africans. Their first objective was Lake Shirwa, which was reported to lie this way. To reach it they had to cross a stretch of mountainous country. It is curious that Livingstone, for the moment, says nothing particular about it; for this is the region we know as the Shire Highlands, in which European settlement has established itself and flourishes today—the "healthy station" for which he had been looking so long. They reached Lake Shirwa at its south-western corner on 18 April. It was the first considerable geographical discovery the Expedition had made. Though unexciting itself, the mountains that surrounded it would clearly be worth examination in the future. And while they were there, they were told of a much greater lake that lay beyond, which stretched so far away to the north that nobody had ever reached its end. They must have been much tempted to go straight on to examine it. But the Manganja, whose territory they were now in, were hostile—they associated a recent drought with the first appearance of the white men's steamer; and in such cases Livingstone found it a good practice to retire from the country after a little while, leaving the people to discover that no ill effects followed their visit, and then to return for a second time later on.

It was a weary business, all the same. Before they could start, they had to go down to the delta to try to pick up stores from a passing ship and to repair the *Ma Robert*. The ship arrived at the end of July, and its captain told them the news of the discovery of Lake Tanganyika by Speke and Burton, marching inland from Zanzibar. "This will surely pull us up to do something more", was Kirk's prompt comment in his journal. It was not until August that they were able to sail again, for the third time, up the Shire, in quest of the great lake to the north.

On this occasion the exploring party was made up of the two Livingstone brothers and Kirk, together with thirty-six Makololo and two guides. "We did not actually need so many," explains Livingstone, "either for carriage or defence; but took them because we believed that, human nature being everywhere the same, blacks are as ready as whites to take advantage of the weak, and are as civil and respectful to the powerful." They followed the course of the Shire closely. They had little trouble from the Manganja, and found that they were an industrious people. Every family with the smallest pretension to wealth grew a patch of cotton, and iron was worked extensively, from ore extracted from the mountains. Some attempts were made to mislead the travellers, with information that the lake they were seeking did not exist; but they overbore all obstruction of this kind, and their pertinacity was rewarded. On 17 September 1859 they discovered Lake Nyasa.

Though they knew nothing of it at the time, another European traveller, Dr. Albrecht Roscher, was approaching the lake at its opposite, northern end. He reached it two months later, and was then murdered on his way back to the east coast.

They found plenty of evidence here of the activities of the slavers, who were raiding to the west as far over as Katanga, and travelled back to the east coast, at Kilwa and Mozambique, by way of the southern end of Lake Nyasa. One party of them, indeed, came to see the explorers. Learning that they were English, they removed hurriedly the same night. Besides slaves, there was also a

89

brisk trade in ivory, malachite, and copper ornaments—for which the metal doubtless came from Katanga. It led Livingstone to believe that if the ivory could be purchased by means of a small steamer on the lake and the River Shire above the cataracts, the slave trade would be made unprofitable, "for it is only by the ivory being carried by the slaves that the latter do not eat up all the profits of a trip". He was convinced—and he had the support of the officers engaged in putting down the slave trade on the East Coast—that "one small vessel on the lake would have decidedly more influence, and do more good in suppressing the slave trade, than half a dozen men-of-war on the ocean".

After a very short stay at the lake, they returned to the ship. For some reason that we do not know, it was at this point that Livingstone made up his mind to dismiss Thornton and Baines from the Expedition. He had been much dissatisfied with them both almost from the start, and he had taken neither of them with him on any of the exploring journeys he had made. He considered that Thornton had "failed in his duties as geologist chiefly from ignorance and a want of energy". But he believed that Baines, as storekeeper, had been "*secretly* making away with large quantities of public property". Accordingly, he now instructed Kirk to travel overland to Tete, taking Rae with him, to search Baines's baggage and then to convey him and Thornton down to the Kongone, where a British ship was due to call in November and would pick them up.

It was a nasty task for Kirk and Rae, and the performance of it almost killed them. No one had visited the country they had to travel through. It turned out to be, at this season of the year, practically waterless. Both men were sick, and though the journey was a short one, lasting only a week, they were totally exhausted by the time they reached Tete. There Kirk performed his unpleasant duty with tact and humanity, and with quite inconclusive results. Baines denied all the charges made against him, and it seems probable that he had been a little careless in his book-keeping—no more. It is also certain that the charges were preferred mainly by Charles Livingstone. His brother accepted them on very unsatisfactory evidence, and almost certainly treated Baines unjustly. The ground of his prejudice against both men was, it seems plain, that they were frequently ill and that they allowed illness to interfere with their work. "Sickness is a thing with which the Doctor has no patience," noted Kirk, most truly, "either in himself or anyone else." But Thornton, as we shall see, was allowed to redeem himself later on; and Baines pursued a remarkable career as an African traveller farther south, in which he had his full share of hardships and showed no lack of spirit in overcoming them.

Having thus purged the Expedition of its two unsatisfactory members, Livingstone felt able to embark on the next part of his task. He had by now secured an adequate knowledge of the lower Zambesi and the problems it presented to navigation; he had similarly explored its main affluent, the Shire, and the potentially important highlands beneath which it flowed; he had matched the work of Burton and Speke by the discovery of Lake Nyasa, the southernmost of the three great lakes of East Africa. It was now time, he thought, to fulfil his promise to the Makololo and to lead them back to their own country. Moreover, he naturally regarded it as his duty to visit the station that was being established there by the London Missionary Society.

The route they took to Sesheke was much the same as that of Livingstone's eastward journey of 1855–1856, except that it followed the Zambesi rather more closely, diverging only at the end for a short distance across the Batoka Highlands. At the Victoria Falls they learnt that the Makololo mission had come to a dreadful end. The leader, Holloway Helmore, his wife, and two children, had died. Their associate, Roger Price, had therefore decided that the mission must be withdrawn, and he lost his wife on the return journey. Livingstone must have been deeply chagrined at this disaster, but his comments on it are entirely charitable. He admitted that Helmore had done all he could, and did not dispute Price's decision to withdraw. He merely observed, with justification, that the catastrophe would not have happened if adequate medical assistance had been available. "It is undoubtedly advisable", he wrote, "that every mission should have a medical man as an essential part of its staff."

They found Sekeletu and his people in a state of the utmost gloom. The chief himself was suffering from leprosy. He believed that his illness was due to witchcraft, and killed off or drove into exile all those who were suspected of having practised it on him. He shut himself up and would admit no one to his presence except one uncle. In these circumstances, the Makololo kingdom was beginning to disintegrate. He consented now to see Livingstone and his companions, and during their visit they were able to do much for the treatment of his disease. He displayed a pathetically intense desire for English settlement in the Batoka Highlands, offering to set aside a defined part of his country for the purpose. For the present, Livingstone could do nothing but express thanks for the offer and promise to consider it further. He had performed his duty to the Makololo, and there was much more to be done elsewhere. After a month at Sesheke, he and his companions began their return journey.

It was Livingstone's last visit to the Makololo. Sekeletu died of his leprosy at the end of 1864; the succession to the chieftainship was disputed; civil war was the consequence, and the tribe, as a political unit, fell to pieces. Livingstone always believed that this was a disaster for the cause he had at heart; that if a strong, well-conducted mission could have been established while Sekeletu's authority was still unimpaired, it might have welded the Makololo into a firm and powerful nation in the deep interior of Africa, a bulwark against the slave trade. For whatever their faults might be (and other Europeans were disposed to view them less favourably than Livingstone), "they did not belong to the class who buy and sell each other, and the tribes who have succeeded them do".

On the journey down the Zambesi, the party decided to attempt the first stage of the Kebrabasa Rapids in canoes. It was a rash experiment and nearly brought death to them all. Kirk's canoe was upset, and he was lucky to escape with his life. Among the baggage he lost were his drawings of plants and eight precious volumes of notes.

They arrived back at Tete on 23 November to find news waiting for them. The government had agreed to Livingstone's request for a new steamer to replace the *Ma Robert*, and it had already been dispatched. More important still, a party of missionaries, sent by the Universities Mission to Central Africa, was on its way, with instructions to establish itself in the highlands the Expedition had found. At last Livingstone and his colleagues could feel that their labours were leading to some practical result. Finally, the government approved a project Livingstone had put forward for avoiding difficulties with the Portuguese on the Zambesi by opening up a new route from the coast to the interior by way of the River Rovuma. That river was under the jurisdiction of no European power—though the Portuguese, hearing of the new plan, made a hasty and unsuccessful attempt to get the Sultan of Zanzibar to recognise it as the frontier between his dominions and theirs.

The next task of the Expedition was clear. It must move down to the coast to await the arrival of the missionaries and the new steamer, trying if possible to combine this with at least a preliminary investigation of the Rovuma. With a sardonic punctuality, as if she knew that she was about to be superseded, on her way down the Zambesi the *Ma Robert* grounded and sank.

On 31 January 1861 the new ship, *Pioneer,* arrived

from England, escorted by a cruiser, carrying some members of the new mission. A week later a second cruiser arrived, with the remainder of the party. They numbered altogether six Europeans and five coloured men from the Cape, headed by Bishop C. F. Mackenzie. Livingstone and Kirk both took to Mackenzie at once : Kirk called him "a trump of a fellow", and Livingstone reported that he "works like a Briton wherever he can". As we have seen, Livingstone approved of the Anglican organisation of the mission. "My experience among missionaries", he wrote to his brother-in-law, "showed a necessity for something of the episcopalian or Wesleyan plan of a superintendent endowed with authority, and of the two the bishop is best." Of the Bishop's colleagues, Horace Waller became a lifelong friend of Livingstone's; but some of the others appealed to him less warmly.

Another missionary accompanied them : James Stewart, "sent out", wrote Livingstone jubilantly, "by the Free Church of Scotland to confer with me about a Scotch colony". Stewart was a young man at the outset of a remarkable career. He quickly became disillusioned about the prospects of colonisation on the lines he had envisaged. Indeed, he came to feel that Livingstone had culpably overestimated the potentialities of the Zambesi country from every point of view, and his journal and correspondence took on a mordantly critical and hostile tone towards the Expedition.

Before conveying the missionaries to their station, Livingstone was anxious to try out the *Pioneer* and the Rovuma at the same time. Accordingly, they made a short experimental trip up the river in March. Its result was encouraging in that the approach from the sea proved to be far better than that to the Zambesi. The new ship, too, was infinitely superior to the *Ma Robert*. But she had one very serious fault : her draught was five feet, and that was two feet too much. Livingstone and his companions spent many weary hours—days and weeks in total—getting her off the shoals she grounded on. Again it was bitterly disappointing, though happily Livingstone did not blackguard the two admirals who had supervised her construction (both of them his warm supporters and admirers) as he had blackguarded the builder of the *Ma Robert*.

After this preliminary trial of the Rovuma, they returned to the Zambesi. The Bishop was impatient to begin his work, and although the Mission and the Expedition were independent, Livingstone undertook to advise him on the choice of a site for his permanent station. As they worked their way slowly up to Chibisa, Charles Livingstone devoted his energies to buying all the native cotton he could. They had had encouraging reports from Manchester on the samples they had previously sent home for examination. Now, though the quantity collected was not great, coming from a necessarily restricted area, it seemed to justify Livingstone's claim that "cotton of superior quality can be raised by native labour alone".

At this point in the *Narrative* of the Zambesi Expedition, with a deliberate effect very unusual in him, Livingstone breaks off to consider the success the party had achieved up to this moment. "Supposing the Mission of the Universities to be only moderately successful," was his conclusion, "a perfectly new era had commenced in a region much larger than the cotton-fields of the Southern States of America." He goes on to explain the reason for his stock-taking : that he regarded this July of 1861 as the turning-point in the fortunes of the Expedition. From now on, as he saw it, their work was constantly frustrated, and ultimately brought to an end, by one enemy above all—the slave trade.

When they got to Chibisa, they soon heard news of the slavers' depredations. They had never before operated so far up the Shire. What was happening was that the Ajawa, a tribe of barbarous warriors living in the highlands, who had long intimidated their neighbours, had now come into touch with agents of the Portuguese dealers at Tete and Quilimane, and were busy raiding and selling off their captives. As Kirk wryly noted in his diary : "We had been the means of opening a slave-hunting country." The day after they started from Chibisa with the missionaries on their way to the highlands, they met a large slaving party face to face. Directly they encountered the Englishmen the drivers abandoned the slaves, without a struggle; and the whole chain of them—eighty-four in all—were freed.

This incident turned out happily, but it opened up formidable problems for the future. It could not be expected that the Portuguese would permit any serious interference with the slave trade. For all the fine words, and perhaps sincere intentions, of their government in Lisbon, the whole colony of Mozambique was deeply involved in it. That was not surprising. The salaries of the officials went unpaid, and there was no "legitimate" industry or commerce out of which they could make a livelihood : unless they were men of exceptionally fine sensibilities, they were almost bound to connive at, or even to take a direct part in, the slave trade.

Other dangers, even greater, lay beyond. The drivers in charge of this party had fled. What would happen if another set stood their ground and defied the Englishmen? And, if more of these slaves were freed in this way, could it be supposed that the Ajawa would remain ignorant and passive? Finally—on a long view the most baffling question of all—what was to be done with the slaves when they had been freed? It was useless simply to release them from their chains, and tell them they were free to go where they chose : that would be most likely to lead them either to a friendless death by starvation or to recapture and a repetition of the misery and terrors of the march into slavery.

Yet mere inaction was impossible. It was unthinkable, on humanitarian grounds, to Livingstone and the Bishop alike. But it would also have been plain folly. For how could the missionaries secure the trust of the people they

96

were settling among if they did nothing to help them against the slave-raiders? Above all, how could "legitimate" trade be given a chance of establishing itself if its protagonists passively allowed the slave trade to continue side by side with it? The slave trade offered easier money: in unfettered competition, as experience in West Africa had shown, it drove out all other trades.

Very soon the problem was put in an even sharper form. A Manganja chief invited the Bishop to establish his mission with him at Magomero, a dozen miles west of Lake Shirwa. With Livingstone's approval, the invitation was accepted. But the Bishop was anxious, before settling down to the work of building the station, to meet the chief of the Ajawa and to try to persuade him to abandon his depredations in favour of peaceful trade. From what was known of the Ajawa, the venture was bound to be dangerous, and it was most unlikely to lead to any useful result; but, as Christians, Mackenzie and Livingstone felt obliged to try the effects of peaceful persuasion, in the face of whatever discouragement or personal risk. On 22 July news reached them that the Ajawa were close at hand and burning a village they had raided. Leaving the rescued slaves in charge of one of the missionaries, "we moved off", says Livingstone in his matter-of-fact way, "to seek an interview with these scourges of the country". That afternoon they met the scourges, returning with their captives and plunder. Unluckily, some of the Manganja in the white men's party set up a war-cry; and the Ajawa therefore (as Livingstone candidly recognises, with good reason) paid no attention to the demand for a parley. Instead, they encircled the strangers and began firing poisoned arrows at them. They also boasted four muskets, and at last Livingstone and his friends were forced to return their fire. As soon as they saw the superiority of rifles, the Ajawa retreated, shouting threats that they would return and kill their enemies as they slept.

As a military action, it was nothing; but it was a sad

day for Livingstone, for he had never fired a gun at an African before in his life. It meant an immediate end to the Bishop's ideas of peaceful persuasion : the new settlement at Magomero would have to be prepared to defend itself from the outset. But he faced the unpleasant truth and set to work at once to make all he could of the station, with the help of the liberated slaves, whom he invited to settle there. He also made it clear to Livingstone that he might presently think it his duty to go to the rescue of the Manganja and drive the Ajawa out of the country. Livingstone's advice was firmly against this plan : "Do not interfere in native quarrels." But it could be advice, nothing more. The Bishop was in control of the mission, and it was time for Livingstone to get back to his proper task of exploration.

His plan now was to resume the examination of Lake Nyasa, in a boat to be carried overland past the Murchison Cataracts, and then to go down to the coast, where they were to meet the Bishop's sister and Mary Livingstone, who was coming up from the Cape to join her husband.

They reached the lake on 2 September and spent eight weeks on it, Livingstone and one party skirting the western shore on land, his brother and Kirk in the boat. The heat was torrid, except when storms blew up, which lashed the waters of the lake into fury; they lost part of their baggage in a night robbery; the people were disagreeable and unco-operative, largely because they were intimidated by the predatory Mazitu, who lived on the high ground to the west of the lake. "The shores are covered with skulls," wrote Kirk in his diary, "and where a foraging party has passed, fresh bodies beginning to decompose lie scattered on the sand." They were unable to reach the north end of the lake. But they saw enough to get a general idea of its rather formidable character; and they learnt more of the flourishing Arab slave trade, maintained by a regular ferry-service, conveying the slaves across to the East African coast at Kilwa and the ports of Mozambique. The remedy for this, Livingstone was convinced, was simple : "A small armed steamer on Lake Nyasa could easily, by exercising a control, and furnishing goods in exchange for ivory and other products, break the neck of this infamous traffic in that quarter."

The Expedition reached its base at Chibisa early in November. Shortly afterwards the Bishop arrived, bringing news that disquieted both Livingstone and Kirk. The Manganja had persuaded him to lead an attack on the marauding Ajawa, with the object of driving them away from the country altogether. The Bishop had given his consent only on stringent conditions, designed to prevent the Manganja from acquiescing or taking part in the slave trade themselves. "I thought it right to do all I could", he wrote, "to rid the country of robbers and murderers, and to help the chiefs to drive away an army of invaders. . . . It was striking a death-blow to the slave trade at its heart." They engaged in two fights with the Ajawa and succeeded in their purpose : the Ajawa sent word that they wished peace with the English. But would this success be permanent? If so, the Bishop would be able to feel that the display of force had been justified. If not, it might lead only to further fights, on a bigger scale, for which the Mission, with its half-dozen Europeans, was not equipped. Livingstone's advice had been set aside, and he felt entitled to express his "friendly disapproval" of the Bishop's action; but afterwards he came round to the view that the Bishop had been right to do what he did.

It was time now to go down to the coast. In descending the Shire the *Pioneer* once more grounded, and it was five weeks before they could get her off. During that time the carpenter's mate died of fever. This was the first death that had occurred on the Expedition—the first of a quick, long series.

On 30 January 1862 H.M.S. *Gorgon* arrived off the Zambesi delta, bringing with her Mary Livingstone and a company of new missionaries, together with the steamer that was intended for Lake Nyasa. It was nearly four years since Livingstone had seen his wife. She had grown very stout in the meantime; but, as we have seen, she cared little for hardships, and she greatly disliked being left behind by her husband. It was a deeply happy reunion. She came now in company with four other women, including the wife of one of the missionaries, Mrs. Burrup, and the Bishop's sister—an elderly lady, quite unsuited by infirmity for the trials before her, yet plucky and always game.

Warned by experience and with the health of women to think of for the first time, Livingstone decided to make only a very short stay in the lowlands. Less than a week would, he thought, be enough. In fact, they were there six months. The engines of the *Pioneer* had been grossly neglected, and they now needed complete overhaul. Mrs. Burrup and Miss Mackenzie were gallantly convoyed straight up the river by Captain Wilson of H.M.S. *Gorgon* in his gig. He took his ship's surgeon with him, and Kirk accompanied the party as guide. On 4 March they reached Chibisa, to be met with the news that the Bishop had died of fever. Furthermore, it appeared that the whole station at Magomero was suffering dreadfully, from sickness and shortage of provisions. Thirty of the Africans were reported to be dead. Kirk and Captain Wilson immediately went over, to find that Burrup, too, had died and the morale of the station was getting low. Before long the missionaries abandoned Magomero and moved down from the high ground, closer to Chibisa. Livingstone regarded this as "the greatest mistake they could have made". Two more of them died. All the constructive work of the Mission appeared to have been brought to an end.

But these disasters did not come alone. When Mrs. Burrup and Miss Mackenzie went up to join their Mission, Mary Livingstone remained with her husband. "She was so strong and well," he wrote afterwards, "and

I had got so into the habit of feeling her to be part of myself, that I did not fear but she would hold out." In the middle of April she had an attack of fever at Shupanga, and on the evening of the 27th she died. It was a terrible blow to Livingstone—the worst he ever suffered. His passing reference to her death in the published *Narrative* gives no hint of his anguish: that appears only in his private journal and correspondence. A fortnight later he wrote "for the first time in my life I feel willing to die"; and though that feeling soon passed, the death of Mary left a mark on the whole of the rest of his life. From this point onwards he became grimmer, more rugged, more solitary and unapproachable than he had ever been before. He shut himself up in an inflexible determination that he would continue his work in Africa until God should see fit to bring his own life to an end.

All this began to emerge very plainly in the next journey the Expedition undertook. Livingstone was determined to make another attempt on the Rovuma. If only it were true, as they had been told, that the river rose directly out of Lake Nyasa, then it surely provided the best approach for them to use—well outside the control of the Portuguese. But when they arrived they found the river lower than before, and evidently quite unsuitable, at that season at least, for navigation. It was immaterial to Livingstone. He took no notice of such obstacles : he only forced himself and his companions on. "All he cares for is accomplishing his object at any risk whatever", Kirk wrote. "It is useless making any remark to him. . . . He himself now thinks the river unnavigable." No wonder that in the end he began to think his leader was "cracked". It was the first manifestation of that heroic and terrifying monomania that drove Livingstone through the incredible wanderings of the last six years of his life. In the end even he was forced to put up with defeat on the Rovuma and to order a return to the coast.

It was now evident that Lake Nyasa would have to be approached by way of the Zambesi and the Shire, for all the disadvantages of that route; and the Expedition's energies had next to be concentrated on getting the new ship (which they christened *Lady Nyassa*) launched on the lake. Her journey was to be made in three stages. First she was to be towed by the *Pioneer* up to the Murchison Cataracts. Next she was to be taken to pieces, and a rough thirty-mile road made to ease the task of carrying them along the bank of the Shire. It would then be possible to reassemble the sections, launch her on the upper river, and so sail out into the lake. The first stage was completed and the second begun by April 1863. And then the Expedition began to disintegrate.

Young Thornton, who had rejoined the party with Livingstone's full consent the previous June, died of fever. A week later Livingstone suddenly announced, in his abrupt way, that his brother was going home, and inquired if Kirk would like to go too. Kirk had asked to be released more than once before, but had agreed to remain with the Expedition at Livingstone's request. Now he was suffering acutely, in the aftermath of dysentery, and he felt he could honourably leave. He began his last journey downstream, in company with Charles Livingstone, on 19 May. Of the original band, only Rae now remained with Livingstone.

Meanwhile, the government at home had made up its mind that the Expedition must be recalled. Livingstone himself had previously "come to the conclusion that no good could be done by this Expedition while the subjects of His Most Faithful Majesty were allowed to follow on our footsteps and spoil all by their slave forays, and told Earl Russell this distinctly". The news of the recall reached Livingstone on 2 July, and he at once began to prepare for evacuation. But the ship could not be taken down to the coast until the rains came in December, and he made up his mind to employ the interval in a last examination of Lake Nyasa—even though he could not use the steamer, which was still stuck at the Murchison Cataracts. He hoped to reach the lake's northern end, to discover if any river fell into it from the west, and to learn more about the eastbound slave trade that crossed it. In fact, the trip achieved very little. He did not attain the top of the lake, and though all the information he could collect was of some value, he learnt nothing new that was of major importance.

No more remained to be done but to pack up and depart. But there was still one more blow to fall. The Universities Mission had lost no time in appointing a successor to Mackenzie, and Bishop W. G. Tozer arrived to take up his work in June 1863. Directly he reached the station he decided that it must be moved to a healthier place in the highlands, and he chose Mount Morambala. No reasonable man could doubt the wisdom of that decision, at any rate as a temporary measure. Kirk said roundly that the station was "quite untenable" : Livingstone, as we have seen, had strongly criticised the removal into the lowlands in the first place. But the population on the mountain was small, and there was little scope there for the Mission's work of teaching—which Livingstone thought it had neglected all along. And then, after a further examination of the problem, Tozer decided that the Mission must be withdrawn altogether, to work in another part of Africa. Having considered several possible stations, he fixed upon Zanzibar.

When Livingstone learnt of this decision in December, he became passionately incensed. "I have told the Bishop plainly what I think of the cowardly retreat", he reported at once. His indignation glows with suppressed fury even in the staid published *Narrative* : "Bishop Mackenzie's successor, after spending a few months on the top of a mountain about as high as Ben Nevis in Scotland, at the mouth of the Shire, where there were few or no people to be taught, had determined to leave the country. . . . The Mission, in fleeing from Morambala to an island in the Indian Ocean, acted as St. Augustine would have done, had he located himself on one of the Channel Islands, when sent to Christianise the natives of Central England.

This is, we believe, the first case of a Protestant Mission having been abandoned without being driven away." Ever afterwards Livingstone regarded Tozer and the Universities Mission with a settled contempt, pursuing them with a searing malevolence that is to be explained only by the intensity of his disappointment in them.

His comments on the decision may be accounted for in this way, but, even so, they cannot be justified. Most competent judges, except Livingstone, regarded it as the right one for Tozer to make. Since the first establishment of the Mission at Magomero, the Shire valley had been—as Livingstone himself described—cruelly devastated by slave raids. To remain there would have meant working among a dwindling population constantly in danger of becoming involved in warfare—and Mackenzie's fighting had been bitterly criticised at home. Whatever Livingstone might say, the country was dangerously unhealthy, as the tragic experience of the past two years had demonstrated. Though any missionary must be prepared to die for his cause, it was senseless to waste good lives superfluously. When the Expedition had left, moreover, British ships would cease to call at the mouth of the Zambesi, and all communication with the outside world would come to an end, except by courtesy of the Portuguese. Lastly, Tozer could fairly claim that Zanzibar was a base for the approach to Central Africa at least as good as the Zambesi or the Rovuma : that was clear from the accounts of Burton and Speke, as well as of the experienced Arab traders.

Each of these reasons for the removal was good, and collectively they were overwhelming. But in this matter Livingstone was inaccessible to reason: he was governed by emotion instead. The removal of the Mission meant the defeat of everything he had worked for since 1857, the shutting-up of the Zambesi valley, which the Expedition had just begun to open, its abandonment to the Portuguese and the slavers. The real truth was that the resources of the Expedition and the missionaries were

wholly inadequate for the immense work they had undertaken. But Livingstone could never bear to admit failure,
even inevitable failure. His powers were so much greater
than those of other men, and his confidence in God's
support so complete, that he could make no allowance for
human limitations or recognise that any task was too
difficult to perform.

With this last grievance working like yeast in his mind,
Livingstone led the Expedition into the delta. In the
middle of February 1864 they were taken off by two
British warships. The *Pioneer*, which was government
property, was towed down to the Cape. But the *Lady
Nyassa* belonged to Livingstone himself : she had cost
£6,000, and he needed all the money he could get for
her. He therefore sailed her up the coast to Zanzibar, bent
on taking her across the Indian Ocean to Bombay, the
nearest promising market. The British consul warned him
that he was unlikely to get there before the break of the
monsoon. Characteristically, Livingstone disregarded this
advice and set off in the tiny ship with a crew of four
Europeans and nine Africans on 30 April. They turned
up at Bombay on 13 June—the day before the monsoon
broke. "The vessel was so small, that no one noticed our
arrival."

Chapter Seven

Preparations for the Last Journey
(1864—1866)

LIVINGSTONE found a kind and sympathetic friend
in the Governor of Bombay, Sir Bartle Frere. He, too,
was deeply interested in the problem of the slave trade.
But he was concerned with a branch of it of which
Livingstone as yet knew very little, though he must have
heard something about it at Zanzibar : the trade from
East Africa to the Red Sea and the Persian Gulf. It was
a very old trade indeed—much older than the Arab
dominion over the East African coast, and that stretched
back a thousand years. But as it passed wholly between
Asiatic countries, its existence was hardly known in
Europe. The humanitarians had thought solely of the
Atlantic trade. Now Livingstone began to learn that there
was another slave trade, perhaps of even greater volume,
that made its way north and east from Africa, quite
separate from the familiar trade to the west. Here was the
explanation of the presence of the Arabs he had met in
the interior, and of their confident, knowledgeable statements about the geography of Africa.

The full implications of this discovery did not appear
to him at once. Side by side with it, he learnt other, more
encouraging, news from Frere. The economy of East
Africa was dominated by merchants from the province of
Bombay; and this led him to hope that, with the firm support of its government and the government of India, it
might be possible to develop so great a "legitimate" trade
that the slavers could be driven out of business. The news

determined the direction that his own next journey should take.

Finding no ready purchaser for the *Lady Nyassa*, Livingstone decided to borrow his passage-money and go straight home. He arrived in London on 23 July 1864.

Whatever doubts might have been felt about the handling of the Zambesi Expedition, and whatever reports had been circulated to Livingstone's disadvantage by those who had quarrelled with him, his welcome was entirely cordial. On the very evening of his arrival, Murchison swept him off to a reception at Palmerston's, and at once he had two conversations with the old Prime Minister about the slave trade. Livingstone noted that he was said to be "more intent on maintaining his policy on that than on any other thing". A week more in London—calling at the Foreign Office, visiting Mr. Gladstone, dining with Palmerston—and he was free to go off to Scotland.

He found his old mother failing—she was now over eighty, and she did not know him at first. She died the following spring. But the reunion with his children gave him deep satisfaction. All that marred it was his anxiety about his sons. Tom, the second son, was never strong and had been suffering from congestion of the kidney. Robert, the eldest, who was now eighteen, had inherited, as Livingstone himself put it, "a deal of the vagabond nature from his father", and after wandering out to Natal had crossed the Atlantic and enlisted, under an assumed name, in the Northern army in the American Civil War. The news reached his father now and gravely distressed him—though of course his sympathies were on the same side as Robert's. Before the close of the year the boy died of wounds in a prisoners' camp in North Carolina. Livingstone always felt his responsibility for Robert's erratic career and early death. He thought he should have spent more time with his children, and that duty was more pressing than ever now that their mother was dead. His determination to return to Africa as soon as he could was a hard one to maintain. It may be true to think of him as having dedicated his life to Africa; but it is false to suppose that he found the dedication easy. Only those who saw him with his children in 1864–1865 could realise what that decision cost him.

Besides his private duty to his family, he had a public duty to perform in England. Although he had reported the proceedings of the Zambesi Expedition to the Foreign Office stage by stage, as opportunity offered for sending home dispatches, he felt he must do something more to make the country aware of what the Expedition had done and of the problems that had confronted it. This part of his task he found peculiarly distasteful, in whatever way it was to be performed. Public speaking was truly an ordeal to him—in that respect he had not changed in twenty-five years, since the day when he had fled in panic from the chapel at Stanford Rivers. As for writing a book, he had declared when he was labouring over the *Missionary Travels* that he would rather cross Africa again than write another. In the end, however, he made his report in both forms : in a lecture to the British Association at Bath in September, and in the published *Narrative* of the Expedition.

The Bath lecture was simple and relatively brief. It had two objects : to explain the scope of the work the Expedition had performed, and what he believed to be its value; and to indicate the difficulties that impeded the opening-up of the Zambesi and Shire valleys through the weakness and maladministration of the Portuguese. He was careful not to make any assertion beyond what he knew to be true from evidence he had himself collected. "I have always hated putting the blame of being baffled upon any one else," he said, "from a conviction that a man ought to succeed in all feasible projects, in spite of everybody; and, moreover, I wish not to be understood as casting a slur on the Portuguese in Europe . . . who are as anxious to see the abolition of the slave trade as could be desired; but the evil is done by the assertion in Europe

of dominion in Africa, when it is quite well known that
the Portuguese in Africa were only a few half-castes, the
children of convicts [1] and black women, who have
actually to pay tribute to the pure natives." This could
not be agreeable reading for the Portuguese. Livingstone
calculated, quite accurately, that they would attempt an
injudicious reply, which would only strengthen his arguments in the eyes of his own countrymen.

The book that Livingstone thought it his duty to write
turned out to be a very different one from the *Missionary
Travels*. His first intention had been to make it no more
than a pamphlet, chiefly concerned with the enormities of
the Portuguese. But, rightly, he soon decided that this
would not be enough : there were other matters on which
he should make a public report. He therefore compiled
the *Narrative of an Expedition to the Zambesi and its
Tributaries*. On the title-page his brother's name stands
with his own. That is not because Charles had any hand
in writing the book, but because his journal was freely
used in it. Here may be one of the reasons why the book
is so markedly inferior to its predecessor. The *Narrative*
has little of the vigour and sparkle of the *Missionary
Travels,* none at all of its humour. It is a plain tale, clearly
told, but wanting in spirit, apt for pages together to be
dull.

In one sense this only proves how faithful the *Narrative*
is to the events it describes : for those were some of the
leading characteristics of the Expedition itself. But what
gives the book its peculiar flatness is that its author felt
obliged to gloss over the story of the Expedition's quarrels
—though they can be discerned by those who know
where to read between the lines; and to reduce the
account even of its tragedies to a few jejune, almost per-
functory paragraphs. To turn from the *Narrative* to Sir
Reginald Coupland's *Kirk on the Zambesi* is to turn from

---

[1] In reports of the speech (e.g. in *The Times*, 20 September
1864) this word appears as "converts". I am sure Livingstone
actually said "convicts".

a dead story to a living one: a rare example of the superiority of an historian's work, written two generations afterwards, to the first-hand account of a participant.

This is no reflection on Livingstone. Handicapped as he was by the feeling that he must omit all the personal history of the Expedition, he could hardly have written a much livelier account of it. Having told the public all that he thought he could, he invited his favourite daughter Agnes to write "Finis" with his pen, and turned to other, more congenial tasks.

The whole book was written in a somewhat unlikely place: at Byron's Newstead Abbey. The house then belonged to W. F. Webb, whom he had tended in sickness when hunting game in Bechuanaland in 1851. Webb invited him to make the house his home when he was in England, and he stayed there, grinding away at his book for seven months, from September 1864 to April 1865. Needless to say, the memory of Byron made no appeal to him at all ("His character does not shine," he noted quaintly. "It appears to have been horrid"); but the Webbs were kind hosts, he had Agnes at his side, and his friends came down constantly to visit him. For all the weary toil of writing, that winter was a happy one. He must often have looked back to it wistfully in the years of wandering that followed.

It is surprising that Livingstone's residence in England brought so little controversy with it. He had said many hard things—and countless more had been said by his brother on his behalf—about a fair number of people, from Bedingfeld and Baines to Bishop Tozer and the Universities Mission; but none of them involved him in any violent public dispute. Nor did any one venture to criticise the conduct of the Expedition. This seems strange when one remembers the formidable denunciation that was provoked by the failure of the Niger Expedition in 1841, and considers that a similar expenditure of public money had been incurred on behalf of the Zambesi Expedition, with a similarly disappointing result. But it can be explained, in two ways. The loss of life among the members of the Zambesi Expedition was comparatively small, whereas on the Niger it had been dreadful; and this was undoubtedly owing to the medical precautions that Livingstone and his companions carefully observed. Above all, it is a tribute to the unique prestige of Livingstone himself. It was great enough to stand up to failure. A simple and striking illustration of this comes from Dickens. In the forties he had been among the most savage critics of the promoters of the Niger Expedition. He detested such people, venting his feelings about them in the character of Mrs. Jellyby in *Bleak House*. Yet in November 1865, when the story of the Expedition was known, he singled out Livingstone as the sole exception in a general and sweeping condemnation of missionaries.[1]

Concurrently with the writing of the *Narrative*, Livingstone was beginning to make the plans for his next journey. There was no question of another elaborate expedition. The money was not forthcoming, and he himself never seems to have considered it. Looking back on the Zambesi Expedition now, we can see that one of the chief causes of its relative failure lay in the defects of its leadership. In his first journey, Livingstone had displayed the highest powers of handling Africans : on his second it appeared that he was much less successful with Europeans. He was dictatorial and secretive, never discussing his plans with his companions until they issued from him as an order. His judgment of white men lacked the perception, and the charity, he always displayed in judging Africans. It is clear that things were made a great deal worse by the malicious gossip of his brother : but, again, the defects of his judgment appear in his willingness to listen to it. He was certainly wise to plan his new journey on the model of his first.

But he did not altogether reject the idea of taking out a white companion. One of the best of the Universities

[1] *The Letters of Charles Dickens* (1893), 591.

Mission men, the Rev. C. A. Alington, was anxious to accompany him, paying his own expenses, and Livingstone considered this proposal seriously, though with hesitation. "I would rather go alone than take any one untried", he wrote. "I suffered too much from Bedingfeld and Co."—and his knowledge of Alington was little greater than his knowledge of Bedingfeld had been when he had agreed to accept him for the Zambesi Expedition. The companion Livingstone would really have liked was Kirk. He had been a good deal less than gracious in acknowledging Kirk's services while they were on the Zambesi together, and they parted in a strangely chilly atmosphere. But that, like so much else, may have been due to the mischief-making of his brother. After their separation the two men corresponded and, in a letter written from the Murchison Cataracts, Livingstone paid Kirk, shyly and belatedly, the tribute he had deserved so well : "You were always a right hand to me, and I never trusted you in vain." [1]

He did what he could to encourage Kirk to write a book on the scientific results of the Expedition : a task that Kirk never performed, not from indolence but because he felt that the loss of his notes in the Kebrabasa Rapids made it impossible to achieve it satisfactorily. And he told Kirk that he would like his company in Africa again, though he could not see his way to securing him a salary. We do not know what Kirk said in reply, but his rejection of the proposal was definite. It was clearly the right decision for him to take. Much though he admired Livingstone, he had found him a trying companion; and he was far too shrewd to suppose that there would be no more difficulties of the same sort, even if Charles Livingstone were not there. Besides, he had his own career to make. He was willing to return to Africa as a government official; but he had done all the exploration he could afford. Livingstone fully accepted this decision, and set

[1] Livingstone to Kirk, 2 June 1863 : Kirk Papers (Rhodes House, Oxford).

himself to find a suitable post for Kirk.[1]

In the end he went alone. The preparations for the journey were made at a great speed. In the first week of 1865, Sir Roderick Murchison wrote to ask what Livingstone's wishes in the matter were. "Quite irrespective of missionaries or political affairs," he wrote, "there is at this moment a question of intense geographical interest to be settled : namely, the watershed, or watersheds, of South Africa. Now, if you would really like to be the person to finish off your remarkable career by completing such a survey, unshackled by other avocations than those of the geographical explorer, I should be delighted to consult my friends of the Royal Geographical Society, and take the best steps to promote such an enterprise." Livingstone's answer was favourable, though he made it clear that he could not now, any more than in the past, be content with the functions of an explorer only. His letter to Murchison contains an important statement of his ideas on the point : "What my inclination leads me to prefer is to have intercourse with the people, and do what I can by talking, to enlighten them on the slave trade, and give them some idea of our religion. . . . To be debarred from spending most of my time in travelling, in exploration, and continual intercourse with the natives, I always felt to be a severe privation, and if I can get a few hearty native companions, I shall enjoy myself, and feel that I am doing my duty." "I could not consent to go simply as a geographer," he told another friend at the same time, "but as a missionary, and do geography by the way." There could be no better summary of the work he actually performed on his last journey than this modest and simple programme, set down before he started.

Murchison then bent himself to raising the money that was needed. £2,000 was in the end forthcoming : £1,000 from his old friend, James Young, and £500 each from

[1] Cf. letters from Livingstone to Kirk, 21 October and 24 November 1864, 13 February, 24 March, 14 April, and 13 May 1865 : Kirk Papers.

the Royal Geographical Society and the government. Neither of these last two grants could be called generous. The Society may perhaps have doubted, from Livingstone's own letters, how far he was going to undertake purely geographical work. The attitude of the government is explicable, too. It had already spent more than £8,000 on the Zambesi Expedition, which could hardly be said to have brought a commensurate return. But by a grave lapse of tact, the Foreign Office, at the same time, asked Livingstone to accept a roving commission to all the African chiefs from the Portuguese boundary northward to Abyssinia and Egypt, on the understanding that he should receive neither salary nor pension. Livingstone was justly offended. In matters of finance he was very far indeed from grasping; but he thought that with this proposal the government was taking advantage of his good nature, and he resented the reference to a pension because it looked as if he expected one, when in fact he had never even hinted at the idea himself. In his attempt to cover up an office blunder, the Foreign Secretary, Russell, unhappily made things worse.

It was an irony that Palmerston was still Prime Minister and that he had made a private inquiry that winter if there was anything he could do for Livingstone. The characteristic, unworldly reply was that he would like Palmerston to secure a treaty with Portugal, guaranteeing free access to the Shire Highlands. The wish was ultimately fulfilled, in 1891.

His financial resources for the journey were, then, barely sufficient. It has to be remembered that he had no fixed income whatever—not even the exiguous £100 he had once enjoyed as the servant of the London Missionary Society; and that he had to provide for four young children. He made substantial sums from his books, and he could have made a great deal more from writing for periodicals : we hear much earlier of his being offered, and refusing, £1,000 for a set of articles for *Good Words,* and £400 for four contributions to another magazine.

But he brushed these opportunities aside, eager to get back to his real work in Africa. There was only one other way in which he could raise money : by the sale of the *Lady Nyassa*. He had wanted to take her with him, but he was compelled to abandon that idea and to concentrate on disposing of her at Bombay as soon as ever he could get out there.

As usual, the preparations took longer than he expected. When he got home in July 1864 he thought it was for a visit of about four months. In fact, he was not able to leave until August 1865.

His efforts to sell the *Lady Nyassa* at Bombay produced nothing but disappointment. When he found a purchaser, it was only at the wretched figure of £2,300, little more than a third of what the ship had cost him. He invested the purchase-money in an Indian bank. A year or two later it failed. In the end, therefore, he never received a penny for the ship; and though he believed that she had all the merits and none of the defects of the *Ma Robert* and the *Pioneer*, she never had a chance to prove herself by sailing on the great lake for which she was designed. It is just like Livingstone that he met this reverse, serious though it was for him, with no more than a shrug of the shoulders. He regarded it all as God's doing : his bitter remarks were reserved for the doings of men.

There were other things to be seen to at Bombay as well. He learnt a good deal more about East Africa from the merchants who were trading there. They collected a subscription for him, which came to £645; but, though he badly needed all the money he could lay hands on for his journey, he insisted that this sum should be invested for the present and used later on as capital for assisting the "legitimate" trade that was to drive the trade in slaves out of East Africa. With the help of Frere, the Governor, he began recruiting men for his journey, securing a dozen sepoys from the Bombay Marine Battalion, in charge of a *havildar*, or sergeant. He also visited a school that had been established at Nassick for the education of freed

African slaves, and agreed to take with him nine boys who volunteered for the service, partly in the hope that they might get home to their own people. Finally, he had the satisfaction of securing from Frere an appointment for Kirk. The control of British affairs in Zanzibar was at this time divided, by a rather cumbrous arrangement, between the Foreign Office and the Government of Bombay. A new Consul had to be appointed just at this time, and it was decided to promote the Agency Surgeon to the office. On Livingstone's recommendation, Kirk was offered the surgeon's post. He had been at pains to make it clear to Kirk that his efforts in this matter were not altruistic : "It would be a great benefit to me to have you on the coast, so it is not altogether unselfish." [1] He was indeed genuinely pleased. Kirk at once accepted the appointment (to which, almost immediately, the office of Vice-Consul was added), and arrived at Zanzibar not long after Livingstone started on his journey into the interior.

Frere had one further kindness to bestow. It had been decided that the Bombay government should present the Sultan of Zanzibar with a steamship. Livingstone was now commissioned to travel across in her and make the formal presentation. This did him a double service : it indicated to the Sultan the respect in which the government held Livingstone, and it was a delicate way of saving him the expense of his passage. With good reason Livingstone described Frere as "a brick of a man".

This second voyage across the Indian Ocean was a sedate affair compared with the first, in the little *Lady Nyassa*. Livingstone reached Zanzibar on 28 January 1866 and lost no time in performing his official duty. He would have been glad to leave the place straight away, but he had to wait nearly two months for a British warship to convey him down the coast to the mouth of the

[1] On this appointment, see the letters from Livingstone to Kirk of 20 October 1865 and 1 January 1866, in the Kirk Papers.

Rovuma, his starting-point. The delay was peculiarly irksome to him. He detested Zanzibar, its smells and filth and quasi-civilisation. Its slave-market—one of the greatest in the East—was a standing offence to him. And he was in embarrassing proximity to Bishop Tozer: obliged, indeed, to meet him and appear civil on ceremonial occasions.

The Sultan, anxious to stand well with the Government of Bombay, showed Livingstone all the polite attention he could. He readily furnished him with a letter, commending him to the Arabs who recognised his authority on the mainland—a potentially valuable document since, at least in theory, the Sultan of Zanzibar's writ ran inland right up to Lake Tanganyika. Livingstone secured a similar letter of introduction from the head of one of the chief Indian firms in the town to his agents at Ujiji, on that lake, and made arrangements for a supply of provisions to be sent up there for his use when he should arrive.

While he was waiting, the news reached Zanzibar of the murder of Baron von der Decken, a German who had been exploring the River Juba in southern Somaliland. The explanation of it lay quite clearly in the brutality and deceit practised by the Baron in his relations with the Africans among whom he was travelling. Livingstone took an interest in examining the evidence in the case, which demonstrated so strikingly the fatal consequences of failing to treat Africans with the courtesy and gentleness of ordinary civilised intercourse.[1]

At last H.M.S. *Penguin* arrived, and on 19 March Livingstone and his followers set off in her from Zanzibar for the Rovuma.

[1] This passage, which was omitted from the published text of Livingstone's *Last Journals,* was printed by the present writer in the *Journal of the Royal African Society,* xl (1941), 335–46.

Chapter Eight

The Last Journey
(1866–1873)

ON each of the two great journeys that he had previously undertaken, Livingstone had set out with clear, well-defined objectives. In 1852 he proposed to examine the access to the Makololo country from the west and east coasts; he took the Zambesi Expedition out in 1858 to test the navigability of the river for steamers and to explore the highlands that lay to the north of it. The purpose of the third journey was never formulated in the same precise terms. But it is essential to an understanding of its story to grasp the geographical aims that Livingstone had in mind when he set out, and to see how far they changed, and why, as the journey progressed. Otherwise it becomes nothing but a story of prolonged fortitude : heroic, but in rational terms unintelligible.

We have seen already that Livingstone refused to undertake this journey solely as a piece of geographical work. Great though his achievement was as an explorer, he regarded that whole business as no more than the means to a much more important end : the opening-up of Africa to Christianity, to lawful trade and the true benefits of European civilisation. From the letters that have been quoted and from others written at the same time, it is clear that he wished to leave himself as free as possible to move where he liked, in the country to the north and north-west of that visited by the Zambesi Expedition. He placed what must be a deliberate emphasis on the looseness of his plans. But he recognised that three great geographical problems remained unsolved in this region, and he was determined to try to discover the answers to them.

In the first place, though he agreed that Speke had discovered "the main source of the Nile" in Lake Victoria Nyanza, and though Baker had revealed that another arm of the river flowed out of Lake Albert, he would not allow that that settled the whole of the ancient question. How were the lakes themselves fed at the opposite end? Was it possible that Tanganyika and Victoria were connected by a river? Furthermore, though he had himself approached the northern end of Lake Nyasa, he had not reached it. He could not therefore be sure that no river ran out of it to the north to flow into Tanganyika. Secondly, nobody yet understood the formation of the central watershed of Africa. His own journeys past Lake Dilolo in 1854 and 1855 had revealed something of it. But the explorations of the past ten years had emphasised the magnitude and the importance of the problem. Until it was solved, there could be no certainty whatever about the structure of Central Africa. That there was such a great watershed, stretching away to the north, was evident from the existence of the Congo, a vast river flowing into the Atlantic from the east. But very little was known of that river, and the third great problem that occupied Livingstone's mind on this journey was to discover where the Congo rose and, if possible, to trace its course down to the sea.

The third journey was different, then, from the first two in its plan. It differed from them also in its equipment. The journey of 1852–1856 was successfully completed with a party of twenty-seven Makololo and a modest quantity of trade-goods for the purchase of food; the Zambesi Expedition, less successfully, with half a dozen Europeans, a varying number of Africans, and adequate supplies of trade-goods, food, and medicines— not to mention the steamers, which, for all their defects, made it easier to move heavy and bulky equipment. On this new journey, as we have seen, Livingstone took one useful precaution, in arranging for supplies to be sent up to Ujiji to await his arrival. In other respects his preparations were a little happy-go-lucky. It was in keeping with the chief object of the journey, the experimental acquisition of knowledge about Africa, that he decided to take with him a number of camels, buffaloes, and mules imported from India, in the hope that some of them might prove immune to the bite of the tsetse-fly—which is not found there. The sepoys whom Livingstone had engaged at Bombay were accustomed to managing these animals: it was one of their chief recommendations. But just as in 1858 he had picked his European colleagues on quite insufficient knowledge of their characters and suitability for the task before them, so now in 1866 he acquired his Indian and African porters without really knowing how they would stand up to the stiff work they would have to face. The sepoys were said in Bombay to be faithful; and so no doubt they were, under the military discipline they were used to, and in their own country. It was impossible to predict how they would behave on a long journey in Africa. The Nassick boys represented another experiment. True, they were natives of the country in which Livingstone proposed to work. But they had been sold into slavery, freed, taken across to India, and put to school there. There was no knowing what effect these upheavals might have had on them. Their characters might stand well in the school at Nassick; that did not necessarily mean they were suitable porters for Livingstone. In fact, there were only two men he could feel quite sure of in advance : Chuma and Wikatani, who had been among the captives freed by Bishop Mackenzie, had served the Mission faithfully, and then, when it was broken up, had gone across to India with Livingstone in the *Lady Nyassa*. At Bombay they were looked after by Dr. Wilson of the Scottish Free Church Mission, who thought very highly of them. They could certainly be relied upon to do their duty.

Livingstone picked up some more Africans at Zanzibar, including three—Susi, Amoda, and Musa—who had served on the Zambesi Expedition. But, again, the rest were somewhat haphazardly assembled. Ten of them came, like Musa, from the island of Johanna, farther south. The reputation of Johanna men was very far from good : Burton expressed his astonishment that Livingstone should have engaged them. And last of all, immediately before he set off for the interior, an Indian trader at Mikindani secured twenty-four more Africans for him.

In that party of sixty men, Livingstone could feel sure of only five—and one of them turned out a scoundrel. He recognised that it was an experiment, cheerfully remarking that if it did not answer he would turn south and secure a party of the well-tried Makololo—rather as if that were as simple an operation as walking into a registry-office in England to engage a new set of domestic servants. One cannot help recalling his remark about the *Ma Robert* : "to build an exploring ship of untried material was a mistake". Surely it was an equally serious mistake for him to enlist a large, ill-assorted party of un-proved porters for the long journey he was now beginning?

For it must be remembered that he was wholly de-pendent upon them. As long as the animals survived, they could take some share of the burdens that had to be carried; but their employment was purely experimental, and it was impossible to count on them. The main work of carrying the baggage had to be performed by the porters. Their good or bad behaviour, their skill or stupidity, determined everything : the speed at which the party moved, its relations with the people it met, the care of its precious medicines and equipment. Livingstone could inspire and encourage his men by his leadership. But he could do no more; for he was in their hands.

It was three days' sail down to the Rovuma. When they got there, it appeared that the mouth of the river had changed its formation a good deal since Livingstone's previous visits through the shifting of sand-banks, and they decided accordingly to land at Mikindani, a small port some twenty miles up the coast to the north. Directly they had disembarked, H.M.S. *Penguin* left, and with her the last white men, with one exception, whom Livingstone ever saw.

The preparations at Mikindani took a fortnight. Livingstone's journal here shows a touching excitement at the prospect of starting off into Africa again : "The effect of travel on a man whose heart is in the right place is that the mind is made more self-reliant; it becomes more confident of its own resources—there is greater presence of mind. The body is soon well-knit, the countenance is bronzed, and there is no dyspepsia. Africa is a most wonderful country for appetite, and it is only when one gloats over marrow bones or elephant's feet that indigestion is possible."

They started on 7 April. The first week was spent in a cross-country march to the Rovuma, through dense jungle, in a "steamy, smothering air". When they reached the river they marched along its banks for three months, and then, being short of food, in a country largely depopulated by slavers, they turned south-west to the town of a chief named Mataka, where provisions were reported to be plentiful. Very little time was needed to discover that the experiment with the animals was unlikely to succeed. They encountered the tsetse-fly on the first day of their march, and it soon appeared that the buffaloes were susceptible to its bite. But with the camels and mules no satisfactory test could be made : for the sepoys treated them with such revolting and calculated cruelty that they were soon almost too weak to carry any burdens at all. They beat one camel to death with the butt-ends of their muskets; it was their usual practice to leave the animals fully loaded in the glaring sun while they sat down to their meals. No beasts could stand up to such treatment, and before long they had all died.

The sepoys, indeed, quickly proved themselves an un-mitigated curse, and before the end of May they were refusing to go on. For the moment Livingstone was able to assert his authority over them, but their conduct steadily deteriorated. Presently they began to hire passing Africans to carry their loads for them, who presented Livingstone, very naturally, with the bill. In the middle of July they were paid off and allowed to return to the coast. The *havildar* for the moment remained, but in the end he turned out as bad as the rest, shamming ill, steal-ing, and selling off his ammunition, and in September he departed too.

The Nassick boys were not much better. Before ever he left the coast, Livingstone was noting that some of them "have the slave spirit pretty strongly". He was willing to blame that spirit for their shortcomings, and to believe that they were further contaminated by their association with the vicious and contemptible sepoys. But whatever the cause, the results of their misconduct were serious. They were lazy, they shirked their tasks, they were in-corrigible dawdlers. The rate of progress was, as always, far slower than Livingstone expected. When he reached Mataka's, where he spent a fortnight at the end of July, he found the place pleasant enough to be likened to Magomero; but it led him to make a bitter comparison between the months it had taken him to arrive there and what he euphemistically described as the "three weeks' easy sail up the Zambesi and Shire".

The endless difficulties with his companions no doubt help to account for the character of his journal. It alters very quickly. There are no more buoyant, ringing pas-sages like the one in which he expressed his delight at the outset. Nor is there much very close observation of the people and their ways—at any rate in comparison with what is to be found in the *Missionary Travels*. The writ-ing is steady, clear, rather toneless. The change is not to be accounted for by ill-health. He had his share of it, but —even allowing for some reticence on the subject—it was far less hampering in these early months than it had often been before. What does most to explain it is, once again, the slave trade : 'the constant, sickening repetition of horrible sights on his way.

It might be supposed that, after what he had already seen and described of the slavers' atrocities in the Shire and Zambesi valleys, there was not much more to be said : that he would have thought it sufficient to note the grim evidence of slaving wherever he found it, without recording the details. That might have sufficed some travellers, but not Livingstone. For one thing, what he was now seeing, for the first time on a big scale, was the Arab slave trade, passing up through Zanzibar to the Red Sea and the Persian Gulf. And he felt bound to describe what he saw, in the hope that Englishmen might ultimately hear of it; for that, he knew, was the only way in which it would be brought to an end. There is nothing morbid about his descriptions, nothing in the least like gloating. Nor does he rail at the slave-traders. It is all set down in terse sentences, with one sad, weary implication : as long as the slave trade is permitted, he says all the time in effect, its necessary consequences will be these.

Even today, when we are growing accustomed to atrocities that the Victorians never dreamt of, these passages in Livingstone's *Last Journals* leave a permanent impression on the mind, especially when they are driven home by the crude and powerful engravings that accompany them. "We passed a woman tied by the neck to a tree and dead, the people of the country explained that she had been unable to keep up with the other slaves in a gang, and her master had determined that she should not become the property of anyone else if she recovered after resting for a time. . . . On asking why people were seen tied to trees to die as we had seen them, they gave the usual answer that the Arabs tie them thus and leave them to perish, because they are vexed, when the slaves can walk no farther, that they have lost their money by

them."[1] These are only simple illustrations of the horrors
he witnessed almost every day. Behind them, as he knew,
there lay a greater and more terrible tragedy : the spread
of civil war, like a prairie fire, through Central Africa,
one people preying on the next to sell its captives to the
slavers. At every possible opportunity on this journey he
emphasised to the chiefs he met that they bore no less
responsibility than the Arabs for the murders that were
done : if they resolutely refused to sell men to the traders,
the trade would be brought to an end. Many of the
Africans he spoke to in this way seemed genuinely
astonished at his reasoning. "At Chensewala's", he noted,
"the people are usually much startled when I explain
that the numbers of slaves we see dead on the road have
been killed partly by those who sold them, for I tell them
that if they sell their fellows, they are like the man who
holds the victim while the Arab performs the murder."
He saw signs, too, that some of his hearers were perturbed
at his condemnation of them. Perhaps these repeated discussions on the long, slow journey might have some effect
in the end.

From Mataka's, continuing in their south-westward
direction, they began to climb, until they reached a height
of over 3,000 feet. A sharp drop then brought them down
to Lake Nyasa, which they reached on 8 August. Getting
across the lake was the next problem. There was a settlement of Arabs not far off, but when Livingstone tried to
make use of the Sultan's letter he found they could not
read, and after consideration they removed their boat to
the opposite side of the lake. Understandably, in view of
his continual denunciations of slaving, they were afraid
of him and mistrusted his intentions : " the fear which the
English have inspired in the Arab traders", he notes
patiently, "is rather inconvenient". Faced with this difficulty, he was obliged to march round the shore of the

---

[1] This was nothing new, or peculiar to the Arabs of East Africa.
The Amalekites treated their slaves similarly: cf. 1 Samuel
xxx. 13.

lake, crossing the Shire once more, where it flowed out at the southern end.

A little farther on, Wikatani met one of his brothers and learnt that another was living near by, together with a sister. He indicated that he would like to stay behind with them. Livingstone felt anxious at parting with him, for fear he might be sold into slavery again : but since the Arabs constantly said that the English attacked the slave trade merely in order to get slaves for themselves and turn them into Christians, he felt it was necessary to consent, to show that Wikatani was indeed perfectly free. The personal inconvenience to him was serious, for it meant the loss of one of the few dependable companions he had. A week later the Johanna men deserted him. An Arab reported that the terrible Mazitu were ahead, and their courage failed. "Musa's eyes *stood out* with terror", and he promptly made off with his compatriots. When he reached the coast he justified his appearance there by stating that Livingstone was dead. The sequel to that tale will appear later on.

These losses reduced Livingstone's band of followers to nine. The men who had gone could not, indeed, be regarded as worth keeping, and the reduced number meant better discipline and perhaps greater speed. But it increased the difficulty of carrying baggage. It much lowered their consequence, too, in the eyes of the people they met, and that helps to explain the privations they now began to suffer. Occasionally, as always, they came upon a chief who was generous by nature, like Kimsusa, who feasted them and gave them more food to take away than the small band could carry. But their usual experiences were very different, mainly because of the depredations of the slavers and the Mazitu, and the consequent suspicion with which these new visitors were received.

Having skirted the southern end of Lake Nyasa, Livingstone wanted to move northward. But his men were too much alarmed at repeated rumours of the presence of the Mazitu in that direction, and he had to be

content with a westerly march until the last week of
October, when at length he managed to turn north-west.
They were, as he rightly surmised, moving along the
watershed between the Lake and the River Loangwa to
the west—through the country where Fort Jameson now
stands, on the borders of Nyasaland and Northern
Rhodesia. In the middle of December they reached the
Loangwa and crossed it. The next stage of their march
brought a crucial disaster.

While they were crossing the watershed, two Yao men
volunteered to join them. They were slaves, but they said
that their masters had been killed by the Mazitu, and this
was confirmed by their chief. Livingstone had no reason
for refusing their offer except his persistent feeling that
the character of every slave was permanently debased by
his slavery. He needed them, and he decided to take
them. They behaved well, making themselves invaluable
as interpreters. On 20 January 1867 they changed loads
with Baraka, one of the most careful men of the original
band; and then, in the forest, they quietly disappeared.
The reason for the manœuvre was easily discovered.
Baraka was of a prudent disposition, and he carried a
small hoard of clothing and beads : his load included five
large cloths, too, with a good market value. But, infinitely
more important, that load also contained Livingstone's
medicine-chest. It was useless to attempt to recover the
loss, since heavy rain came on and at once obliterated the
footsteps of the fugitives. "I felt as if I had now received
the sentence of death", he wrote in his journal. And indeed, in the long run, he had.

There were only two courses open to him : to return
to the coast for fresh supplies, or to press on, regardless of
his loss. Livingstone does not seem to have considered for
one moment the possibility of returning. And though, in
the light of after-knowledge, that might appear the more
sensible course, there were good reasons against taking it.
His journey to this point had already taken nine months.
Could he really face another nine months, simply to re-

gain his starting-point? Besides, though in his weary trudge he had as yet reached none of his objectives, he felt certain—as he always felt to the very end of his journey—that they could not be far away. And as if to confirm the rightness of his decision, a fortnight afterwards he had an opportunity to send word to Zanzibar by a passing slave-party, explaining his plight and ordering medicines to be dispatched to him at Ujiji.

They were all acutely short of food at the time—"it has not been merely want of nice dishes, but real biting hunger and faintness". A few days later he notes: "in changing my dress this morning I was frightened at my own emaciation". (It was probably the first time in his life that Livingstone had ever written the words "I was frightened".) By March he was beginning to be gravely ill. He kept on his way, however, and on 1 April he felt rewarded by reaching Lake Liemba. The alternative name of this lake, he observed, was "Tanganyika"; but he rejected the idea that it could be an arm of the lake Burton and Speke had discovered, because its altitude was 1,000 feet higher than that given by Speke. "Liemba" is, in fact, the southernmost tip of Lake Tanganyika. Neither measurement of altitude had been correct, but Livingstone's was much nearer the right figure than Speke's. Here he remained a fortnight, largely owing to his extreme weakness: he had "a fit of insensibility, which shows the power of fever without medicine".

It was his intention to continue north-westward up the lake, but again he was frustrated by news of war in his path. Instead, hearing that a party of Arabs had arrived at Chitamba's, a little farther south, he turned to meet them. They at least could read the Sultan's letter. They showed it respect and received Livingstone with courtesy and kindness. They offered to convoy him to Ujiji, but he insisted that he must go on west, to find the reported Lake Mweru and to examine the watershed further. This was bound to be difficult, for the state of the country in that direction was extremely disturbed. The Arabs advised him to wait until they could secure some further information, and use their influence to make peace. There was nothing Livingstone liked less than waiting. It was idleness, he repeatedly said, that really made him ill. But the Arabs convinced him that it would be foolishly dangerous to go on in his chosen direction, and as he would not give up his objective, he could do nothing but wait, much though it irked him.

In the end he spent over three weary months at Chitamba's, followed by two more months' very slow marching in company with some of the Arabs, and recompensed in the end by the discovery of Lake Mweru, on 8 November 1867. "Discovered" may not be a precisely accurate word, for the Portuguese traveller Lacerda had visited this region in 1798, and a traditional account of his coming survived there. But no full narrative of his travels had ever been published in England,[1] and for practical purposes Livingstone's description of the country was the first. To the south of the lake the dominant ruler was called Casembe, as he had been in Lacerda's time—"Casembe" being a title, not a personal name. Livingstone at once went to visit the reigning Casembe, an unprepossessing, brutal, but—as it afterwards appeared—honourable chief; and here, again, he had to submit to an exasperating delay. He occupied part of his time in writing a long official dispatch home. He never actually sent it, for want of paper; but it survives in his journal. In it he set himself to summarise the results of his travels up to this point.

The discovery of Lake Mweru was not in itself any great thing to show for the labours of a year and three-quarters. But his examination of this country was beginning to lead him to an important geographical theory of the water-system of the whole region. It looked as if it was all drained by one great river, which at first flowed south and then bent round to the north, making its way

[1] Richard Burton printed a translation of Lacerda's brief diary of his journey in *The Lands of Casembe* (1873).

through two substantial lakes *en route*. The theory was based largely on hearsay, and it might yet prove wrong. The great river seemed, oddly, to bear three different names in its course—Chambesi, Luapula, Lualaba; he had as yet seen only one of the lakes for himself; and even if he could prove this idea to be right, he had no notion of the lower course of the river or how it might reach the sea. The most useful thing he could do immediately was to find the second lake, Bangweolo, which was reported to lie to the south of Casembe's territory. He would have liked to set out on this quest at once, but the rainy season had begun and Bangweolo was said to be particularly unhealthy. Deprived of his medicine-chest, even he felt it would be unwise to go on. Accordingly, he decided to march north-east, trying to reach Ujiji and pick up what was waiting for him there. But his path was blocked by flooding, and he had to return. In April 1868 there was a further movement of desertion among his men, covertly encouraged by one of the Arab slave-traders with whom Livingstone was supposed to be on good terms. It made no difference. He went on with his work, with five men only.

His journey to Lake Bangweolo began on 1 June, in company with the same trader, who wished to go south-west to Katanga, to buy some of the copper for which that district was already well known. Casembe offered no opposition, though he thought it right to warn Livingstone in advance that Bangweolo was "only water—nothing to be seen"; and on 18 July he reached the lake. He made a short trip on it, visiting one or two of its islands and satisfying himself about the point at which the Luapula entered it. He also wrote a careful account of the great "sponges", or bogs, that abounded in this country and formed a stiff obstacle to movement, even when the dry season was well advanced. They occurred at intervals of about a mile, and in crossing them the traveller was liable to be plunged suddenly into holes, waist-deep, waterlogged, and full of leeches. "When one plumps therein", he notes, "every muscle in the frame receives a painful jerk." Except to the curious geographer, Bangweolo had no attractions to offer at all.

As he returned northward, he found the country in a state of the wildest disorder, Casembe and a neighbouring chief having combined to drive out the Arabs. Livingstone managed to hold aloof from the quarrel, but again it meant a delay of months. It was not until 11 December that he was able to set off, with one of the Arab parties, for Ujiji.

The year 1869 opened badly, with a heavy attack of pneumonia, the consequence of repeated wettings. Mohammed Bogharib, the slave-trader he was travelling with, was as kind as could be, and arranged for him to be carried—for the first time in his life, as he ruefully noted; but the jolting motion, under the merciless sun, was painful in the extreme. They reached Lake Tanganyika on 14 February. The usual slow negotiations then began for hiring canoes, followed by a fortnight's sail across and up the lake. It was not until 14 March that they arrived at Ujiji.

When he got there, Livingstone immediately found that almost all the goods sent up for him from the coast had disappeared or had never arrived. Most important, the medicines were said to be still at Unyanyembe, a fortnight's march away to the east. He records this discovery without the least emotion. He makes nothing at all of his dreadful disappointment, merely expressing thankfulness that a little had been saved : "I found great benefit from the tea and coffee, and still more from flannel to the skin."

Here again, at Ujiji, Livingstone had a clear choice of courses before him. He quickly found that there was no believing the tale that his medicines were near at hand. But, assuming that the consignment had been lost or pilfered, it would still be possible for him to return easily to Zanzibar : for the road was well known as one of the chief highways of trade in East Africa. At Zanzibar he could pick up the medicines and supplies he wanted and come back at once. It need not mean a very long delay. The argument for a return to Zanzibar now was far stronger than it had been when the medicine-chest was lost. It was a much shorter and easier journey; he already had a substantial achievement behind him, whereas then he felt that he had as yet done nothing; he had been very seriously ill, and he must have known that even his constitution could not stand such strains for ever. But as on the previous occasion, so now, the journal shows no hint that he considered such a course. Sir Reginald Coupland has described Livingstone's failure to go back to Zanzibar immediately his medicines were lost as, "in the long run, suicidal". There were weighty arguments against a return then; but the phrase could justly be used to describe his refusal to go back from Ujiji now.

Was the decision due to a kind of infatuation, a mystic feeling (which did undoubtedly possess him) that it was his duty to go travelling on through Africa until God determined that his task was done? There were perhaps other, more rational, explanations of it as well. Though these supplies had miscarried, he must have thought that it would be an easy matter to get them replaced. Ujiji would be the base for his next operation, and he would be able to get back there much more quickly to pick them up. Moreover, even if the journey to Zanzibar and back was a relatively simple matter, the time spent on it was, from his point of view, totally thrown away : the road had already been described by Burton and Speke, and other travellers would undoubtedly follow their trail. Economy of time, on the other hand, was a matter of great importance to Livingstone. To appreciate that, one must remember the smallness of his resources—those skinny grants from the government and the Royal Geographical Society. A great deal of his money had already been spent, much of it wasted through theft and loss. To go down to Zanzibar and back would be a costly operation, in money and time. He could afford neither.

And so he contented himself with a burst of writing : at the end of April he records that he has already written forty-two letters. In the relative comfort of Ujiji he was beginning to recover his health, and after a two months' rest he was impatient to start out again, across the lake and over into Manyuema beyond, where there were said to be many rivers—no doubt the rivers he was seeking.

It was not merely his old, constitutional dislike of remaining still that made him so anxious to be off. He loathed Ujiji. "A den of the worst kind of slave-traders", he called it. He likened them to the Portuguese half-castes he had met on the Zambesi, distinguishing them from the Arabs he had lately been travelling with, whom he once called "gentlemen slave-traders". The distinction was not based on the personal kindness that his recent companions had shown him. Like the Zambesi traders, the Ujijians were mostly half-castes, part Arab, part African. They had no conception of genuine trade at all, even in slaves: "It is not a trade, but a system of consecutive murders; they go to plunder and kidnap, and every trading trip is nothing but a foray." They knew nothing about fair dealing. The half-caste to whom Livingstone's goods had been consigned, Thani bin Suelim, was away when he arrived, and it was two months before he shuffled up. When he did, it became clear to Livingstone at once that he was in the hands of an extortionate, twisting scoundrel. It was only after much haggling that he consented to take charge of the precious packet of letters for the coast. Livingstone had grave misgivings about their safe arrival. Rightly, for not one of them was ever heard of again.

In this hateful place he was detained four months. It was said to be impossible to travel in Manyuema until the floods went down, and he did not get off until 10 July. Geographically he had one plain objective : to "trace down the western arm of the Nile to the north—if this arm is indeed that of the Nile, and not of the Congo". More important, he was embarking on a journey into a country that was totally unknown. Wild tales ran about Ujiji that the people were cannibals. But no one knew: for no one had ever described Manyuema whose word could be trusted. It was only at this moment that the Arab traders were beginning to penetrate the country, in search of ivory and slaves; and none of them had been beyond Bambarre, the seat of the principal chief in the eastern part of the country.

Once again Livingstone joined up with Mohammed Bogharib. Across the lake the journey lay through a mountainous country, and he at once began to find that, since his pneumonia, he could no longer climb as he had once done. It was a slow and exhausting journey. The party reached Bambarre on 21 September : seventy-three days to perform what Livingstone calculated was eighty hours' actual travelling.

The attitude of the Manyuema to the visitors was civil, but puzzled and suspicious. They could not understand the value that was set upon the ivory of their elephants, and thought this was a trick for plundering them. Livingstone understood their anxiety very well : "We light on them as if from another world : no letters come to tell who we are or what we want. We cannot conceive their state of isolation and helplessness." Having rested a little while, he went on westward again, without the slave-traders, to try to reach the River Lualaba and sail down it in a canoe. But he found himself balked by his old enemy : slave-traders had just preceded him into the country, and the people would not believe but that he was one of them. Finding that he could make no progress in these circumstances, he returned to Bambarre and at the end of 1869 set off again, in a more northerly direction, in company with Mohammed Bogharib. He gave a vivid account of his journey this winter in a later dispatch to Lord Stanley :

"The country is extremely beautiful, but difficult to travel over. The mountains of light grey granite stand like islands in new red sandstone, and mountain and valley are all clad in a mantle of different shades of green. The vegetation is indescribably rank. Through the grass —if grass it can be called, which is over half an inch in diameter in the stalk, and from ten to twelve feet high— nothing but elephants can walk. . . . The rains were fairly set in by November; and in the mornings, or after a shower, these leaves were loaded with moisture which wetted us to the bone. The valleys are steeply undulating, and in each innumerable dells have to be crossed. . . . By placing a foot on each side of the narrow way one may waddle a little distance along, but the rank crop of grasses, gingers, and bushes cannot spare the few inches of soil required for the side of the foot, and down he comes into the slough. . . . Every now and then the traders, with rueful faces, stand panting; the sweat trickles down my face, and I suppose that I look as grim as they, though I try to cheer them with the hope that good prices will reward them at the coast for ivory obtained with so much toil."

Such travelling would soon have exhausted the fittest man. Livingstone had repeated attacks of fever, and at Mamohela, "quite knocked up and exhausted", he decided that, for the present, he could not go on. He remained there from February to June 1870.

While he was at Mamohela, he heard that Musa and the Johanna men had reported at the coast that he was dead and that the government and the Royal Geographical Society had combined to send out a party under E. D. Young, who had known Livingstone—and Musa —on the Zambesi Expedition, to test the truth of the story. Quickly and efficiently, Young had made his way up by the Zambesi to Lake Nyasa, and there he had soon secured proof that Musa's tale was pure invention, with an obvious motive behind it. Livingstone was touched and grateful: especially, no doubt, because it showed the value that the government and the Society set upon his work, for all their earlier niggling.

When he prepared to move forward in June, he was

faced by another desertion. Only three of his men would accompany him. His resolve was inflexible : he would go, then, with only three. But it soon appeared that he had mistaken the direction of the river he sought, and he was forced to limp back to Bambarre. It was literally limping, for he was suffering dreadful pain from ulcers in his feet. He had never had them before, though "the wailing of the poor slaves with ulcers that eat through everything, even bone, is one of the night sounds of a slave-camp". No remedy seemed to help until, under advice, he tried the application of malachite. It was ten weeks before he could think of moving, and then he was forced to remain where he was for want of men.

In the end he was detained at Bambarre for seven months. He spent much of the time in reflecting on the geographical problems he had still to solve. It is at this point that his quest for the sources of the Nile begins to take on what may be called a mystical character. His mind constantly reverted to the account of it that the Ancients had given, above all to the words of Herodotus, noted down from a scribe in Egypt: "Between Syene and Ele-phantine there are two hills with sharp conical tops; the name of the one is Crophi, of the other, Mophi. Midway between them are the fountains of the Nile, which it is im-possible to fathom. Half the water runs northward into Egypt, half to the south towards Ethiopia." Reports reached him of "fountains", or springs, from which rivers took their rise in Katanga, not very far away; and between two of these springs, he learnt, there was a remarkable great mound. Perhaps, after all, the account given by Herodotus in the fifth century B.C. was correct. Could he prove it? More fascinating still, he began to believe that he might discover "evidence of the great Moses having visited these parts". (One remembers how, not long after-wards, Gordon spent nearly a year in Palestine, searching for the sites of episodes in the Bible.) But these exciting speculations were accompanied in his mind by grave pre-sentiments for the future. His attack of pneumonia, long and increasingly serious bouts of fever, the ulcers in his feet, he wrote, "warn me to retire while life lasts".

That prudent decision was one he could not take. He chose instead to endure the torment of inaction, waiting for the opportunity, which he was sure would come, to recruit the men he needed and march on. At the end of January 1871, news reached him from Zanzibar by the traders: there had been a great epidemic of cholera there, and 70,000 people were said to have died of it. A week later, ten men arrived, sent up for him by Kirk.

It was at once clear that they would not be very reliable. They were slaves of the Indian traders at Zanzibar, and Livingstone soon detected the fatal signs of the slave mentality in them. Their first act was to strike for higher wages. Still, they offered him the chance of moving he had so long desired, and a week after their arrival he was off to the west, once again intent on reaching the Lualaba.

His notes of the journey are simple and brief. He was on the move again at last, but travelling had none of its old tonic effect on him. "I am heartsore, and sick of human blood," he exclaims at one point; and then, after his men had shown signs of mutiny, despair opens up before him—"so many difficulties have been put in my way I doubt whether the Divine favour and will is on my side". It must have seemed to him like a direct answer from God to that cry that on the very next evening they arrived at their goal: the town of Nyangwe, by the great Lualaba, 3,000 yards wide, flowing steadily away to the north.

Nyangwe was a place of note for its market. It was by far the largest Livingstone had seen on this journey, and he studied it with close interest. He was soon able to disarm suspicion and to move about freely, inquiring the names of the things on sale. His account of the market is valuable as one of the clearest pictures we have of African trade untouched by European or Arab influences. It beguiled the time while he was negotiating for canoes, which

were to take him up the river and so make it possible
for him to visit Katanga. But that business was obstructed,
as he soon found out, by the lies his new recruits were
telling about him behind his back : he wanted canoes,
they said, solely to kill men. Their one wish was to return.
At all costs they were determined to thwart his desire to
go on. And they were covertly supported by a slaving
party, which had reached Nyangwe at the same time.
The slavers were always nervous at the reports Livingstone might make of their doings. Again the journal takes
on a desponding tone : "all seems against me", he notes
on 14 July.

The next day this vexation was swallowed up in a
frightful atrocity, which Livingstone never forgot. It was
a market-day, and some 1,500 Manyuema—chiefly
women, as usual—arrived to buy and sell. The slavers
had already involved themselves in a quarrel with the
people on the other side of the river, and some of their
villages were burning. Now, without the least warning,
the slavers suddenly began to fire on the crowds in the
market. As the terrified women rushed for the river to try
to board the canoes there, they were mown down; the
canoes jammed; the only hope of escape was by swim-
ming to the protection of an island a mile away. But it
was upstream, and the current of the river was strong:
very few of the swimmers survived. The slavers themselves estimated that 300–400 people were killed.

What made it more dreadful was that this was the first
time women had ever been attacked on their way to
market here: by an inviolable custom of the country, they
were free to move about for this purpose unmolested, even
during times of civil war. To Livingstone it was the
crowning illustration of the terrible consequences of the
slave trade. Its introduction into Manyuema meant the
end of a well-defined system of public order : it meant,
too, the end of the flourishing, established trade, which
depended on peace. "Oh, let Thy Kingdom come," he
wrote. "No one will ever know the exact loss on this

bright sultry summer morning; it gave me the impression of being in Hell."

He at once made up his mind to abandon his journey to Katanga and to return to Ujiji. Nothing now could induce him to remain in the slavers' company. All along his route he found the country disturbed by their activities: "came through miles of villages all burned", he notes. Not surprisingly, the people were suspicious of him, unable to distinguish him from the slave-traders, and before long he was actually attacked. A spear flung at him very narrowly missed, and two of his party were killed. "We had five hours of running the gauntlet, way-laid by spearmen, who all felt that if they killed me they would be revenging the death of relations. . . . I became weary with the constant strain of danger, and—as, I suppose, happens with soldiers on the field of battle, not courageous, but perfectly indifferent whether I were killed or not." A month of renewed sickness followed, and then his strength returned for the final stretch of the journey. He arrived back at Ujiji on 23 October, to find once again that the goods sent up for him from the coast had been sold off by the trader to whom they had been consigned. "This was distressing", he remarks in his mildest way. When the trader came to call on him, he set him down, in the special category normally reserved in his mind for Baines, as "a moral idiot". One of the best of the Arab traders generously offered to sell off some of his ivory for trade-goods, and present them to Livingstone. But Livingstone could not bear the thought of depending on his charity, and he determined to hold out independent as long as he was able, waiting for what might happen.

What did happen seems like a miracle. On the morning of 10 November 1871, Susi came dashing up to announce that an Englishman had arrived. Going out at this improbable news, Livingstone saw a large party advancing, headed by the American flag. It was, indeed, under the command of a white man, who walked up to

him and said, "Dr. Livingstone, I presume?" " 'Yes,' said
he, with a kind smile, lifting his cap slightly."

The stranger was Henry Morton Stanley. In order to
account for his appearance at Ujiji, it is necessary to go
back a little over the story of his earlier life. Our evidence
for it comes almost entirely from himself, and there is
good reason for suspecting untruth or exaggeration in
much that Stanley wrote. But if even half of his own
account of his early years is true, it is a story fit for a
picaresque novel.

He tells us that he was an orphan, brought up in North
Wales, first by his grandparents and then in the work-
house at St. Asaph. There he suffered so much from the
cruelty of the schoolmaster, James Francis, that he ran
away. He shipped as a cabin-boy to the United States,
worked for a time in and around New Orleans, and was
then swept, in the first fury of the Civil War, into the
Southern army. He was taken prisoner at the battle of
Shiloh, and while in captivity determined to change sides.
He served in the Northern navy, and when he left it at
the end of the war in 1865 became a journalist. In this
profession he quickly made his mark, and in 1868 he
entered the service of the *New York Herald,* the greatest
sensational newspaper of its time. After reporting the
Abyssinian war for the *Herald,* he passed on to the civil
war in Spain. In the autumn of 1869 he was summoned
to Paris to see James Gordon Bennett, Junior, the pro-
prietor of his paper, who commanded him to go and "find
Livingstone". He was to spend whatever money might be
needed, drawing on the *New York Herald* until the task
was completed.

Bennett was not a philanthropist, though he told
Stanley, with kind forethought, to take with him enough
provisions to relieve Livingstone if he was in want. The
reason for sending Stanley on this mission was simple.
The "finding" of Livingstone would be one of the great
newspaper scoops of the world. Bennett showed very

clearly how he thought of the matter when he gave
Stanley his detailed instructions. He was not to go
directly, by any means, in search of Livingstone. First he
was to attend and report the opening of the Suez Canal,
and to write a "practical" guide to Lower Egypt. He was
next to go on to Jerusalem, Constantinople, the Crimea;
to find out what he could about the Russian expedition to
Khiva and the Euphrates Valley Railway; and then to
make his way across to India. If by the time he arrived
there Livingstone had not been heard of, Stanley was to
go across to Zanzibar and travel up into the interior in
search of him. It is well to remember these instructions:
though Stanley did, indeed, set out to "find" Livingstone,
he had a great many other more immediate tasks to perform on the way.

He performed them, and they took almost a year.
When he got to India, in August 1870, he found that no
certain news had been received of Livingstone, and he
accordingly prepared to search for him. But he met with
insuperable delays, at Zanzibar and Bagamoyo. It was
not until 21 March 1871 that he was at last able to start
for the interior, in command of an expedition comprising 192 men.

These delays were not Stanley's fault. Whatever defects
he had, he never showed any want of energy. Once the
party was at last on the march, it moved with a ruthless,
mechanical stride. Stanley would tolerate no delay of any
sort. He used the whip freely; his two white companions,
Farquhar and Shaw, were successively left behind and
died; the great party went on. It was a remarkable feat of
determination and endurance, in violent contrast to the
slowness of Livingstone's movements. But, then, Stanley
was a fierce disciplinarian. The purpose of his march was
quite different: he had no interest in what he saw on the
way—he was travelling to a single end. Above all, he had
ample supplies, of medicines and food and currency.
What can fairly be said of him is that he managed his
expedition—so utterly different from Livingstone's—with

efficiency and tenacious perseverance.

On 3 November he was rewarded by circumstantial news of a white traveller, who could be no one but Livingstone, recently arrived from Manyuema at Ujiji, only a few days' march ahead. On the morning of the 10th the waters of Lake Tanganyika came into sight. About noon he reached Ujiji, and the two white men met.

Stanley's description of the meeting is classical. The greatness of the occasion has awed him into dropping the accustomed flummeries of his style. He tells the story so simply that the scene takes on the sharpness of an etching: once read, it is never forgotten. His account of Livingstone is valuable: "Dr. Livingstone is about sixty years old, though after he was restored to health he appeared more like a man who had not passed his fiftieth year. His hair has a brownish colour yet, but is here and there streaked with grey lines over the temples; his beard and moustaches are very grey. His eyes, which are hazel, are remarkably bright; he has a sight keen as a hawk's. His teeth alone indicate the weakness of age; the hard fare of Lunda has made havoc in their lines. His form, which soon assumed a stoutish appearance, is a little over the ordinary height, with the slightest possible bow in the shoulders. When walking he has a firm but heavy tread, like that of an overworked or fatigued man." This is the last account we have of Livingstone. It tallies well with earlier descriptions and with the singularly consistent series of his portraits—culminating in the splendid photograph of him taken by Thomas Annan at Glasgow in 1864.

Stanley spent four months with Livingstone. The food he brought, and his company and conversation, soon enabled Livingstone to recover much of his health and former spirits. They began to discuss their future plans, and as it appeared that Livingstone wished to examine the north end of Lake Tanganyika, to see if a river flowed into or out of it, Stanley proposed that they should sail up together.

The trip occupied a month, and it enabled them to discover that all the water at the northern end ran *into* the lake. Livingstone continued, none the less, in the firm belief that there was some outlet. It was no longer possible to hold that the water flowed out by a river northward into Lake Albert, and so into the Nile. Instead, Livingstone began to suppose that the outlet was on the west side, into the Lualaba. If anything had been needed to stiffen his resolve to pursue his examination of the country through which that river ran, this discovery would have supplied it. But his mind was, in truth, made up. Stanley put before him all the arguments in favour of returning home, to recuperate from his privations, to get proper dental care, and to see his family. They were strong arguments—the last of them much the strongest of all; but he swept them aside in favour of another journey "due west to the ancient fountains". If there was a touch of monomania in this, Livingstone was yet aware that his whole theory, for which he was jeopardising his life, might well be wrong : "The medical education," he wrote, "has led me to a continual tendency to suspend the judgment. . . . I am even now not at all 'cock-sure' that I have not been following down what may after all be the Congo."

They arrived back at Ujiji on 13 December, and Livingstone began at once on the task of writing a long series of letters home, which Stanley could take back with him. For the first time, he felt some security that letters he wrote from Ujiji would reach their destination. He had—and with good reason—the utmost faith in Stanley's efficiency and zeal, in marked contrast to what appeared to him to be the negligence of the British consulate at Zanzibar. This is not the place for a full discussion of the thoroughly unpleasant controversy into which he now plunged : it has been examined with meticulous care by Sir Reginald Coupland in *Livingstone's Last Journey*. Briefly, Livingstone now came to believe that Kirk, the Vice-Consul at Zanzibar, on whom he had mainly depended to organise his communication with the outside world, had let him down; that the depredations and delays he had suffered from were Kirk's fault, since he was responsible for engaging the porters and their leaders; that Kirk, in short, had taken no trouble on his behalf at all. His mind seems to have been poisoned by Stanley, who had clearly disliked Kirk on sight—he was the very type of quiet, reserved Englishman whom Stanley found it most difficult to handle. But Stanley must not bear the whole blame. Once the idea of Kirk's disloyalty had entered his mind, Livingstone seized upon it, and it took such a firm hold there that it could never quite be dislodged. It did not occur to him in this instance to exercise his "continual tendency to suspend the judgment", to wait until he could hear what Kirk had to say—and there was so much to be said that in the subsequent inquiry, made on the government's behalf by Sir Bartle Frere, Kirk was exonerated from the smallest blame. Livingstone chose instead to listen to Stanley and to jump to conclusions. It was Baines and Bishop Tozer all over again. Psychologically, the explanation is evident : they were all scapegoats for the failure of projects on which Livingstone had set his heart—projects that failed, in reality, because they were beyond his powers, or any man's, to achieve with the resources at his disposal. But there is this important difference : that Baines and Bishop Tozer were mere associates, where Kirk was one of his staunchest friends. In the bitterness of his anger now, Livingstone wrote things to Kirk, and to other people concerning him, that he should never have done without much fuller knowledge; and, worse still, he discussed Kirk with Stanley, who went home to Europe and in his first public speech said he had "a mission from Dr. Livingstone to describe Kirk as a 'traitor' ". So the misunderstanding and rancour continued; and though Livingstone learnt some of the truth later on and softened towards Kirk a little, he never realised the magnitude or the cruelty of his error before he died.

After a fortnight's further stay at Ujiji, the travellers moved off towards the east. It was their plan to go together to Unyanyembe; that Stanley should then press on to Europe, while Livingstone waited for the porters that he would send up from the coast. When they arrived, he would be able to set off again on his westward journey.

They parted at Unyanyembe on 14 March 1872. Livingstone's feeling for Stanley was one of simple, unalloyed gratitude. Stanley's company, and the material help he had brought, had given him fresh heart for his work, a good chance of completing it. He expressed his thanks in letter after letter—to the British government, to his friends, to James Gordon Bennett. He cannot but have noticed some of Stanley's faults. Stanley himself records three occasions on which Livingstone restrained his somewhat ready violence towards Africans. But whatever he thought, his gratitude prevented him from writing a single word in Stanley's disparagement.

Stanley, on his side, was profoundly and genuinely impressed by Livingstone. Reading his book eighty years afterwards, it is not always easy to realise that. "It is, without exception", wrote Florence Nightingale, "the very worst book on the very best subject I ever saw in my life." [1] The language of sensational journalism becomes irretrievably dated, and that is the language of *How I Found Livingstone*. It gives a tawdry, cheapjack appearance to the whole story: worse still, it leads the reader to question his sincerity. But on this point there can be no doubt at all. Stanley's admiration for Livingstone was constant and unstintedly expressed—for his fortitude, his intellect, above all for his moral character. "For four months and four days", he wrote, "I lived with him in the same house, or in the same boat, or in the same tent, and I never found a fault in him. I am a man of a quick temper, and often without sufficient cause, I dare say, have broken ties of friendship; but with Livingstone I

[1] Sir E. Cook, *The Life of Florence Nightingale* (1913), ii. 315.

never had cause for resentment, but each day's life with him added to my admiration for him." He proved his words sincere when he took up Livingstone's work after his death.

It was now his immediate business to return to Europe and proclaim that Livingstone was "found". When he reached Bagamoyo he met another "relief expedition", sent out by the Royal Geographical Society to aid Livingstone, preparing to start for the interior. Among its members was Livingstone's youngest son Oswell. As it appeared that their work had already been performed, they turned back. The sensation that Stanley created when he arrived in Europe was as great as he, or his paper, could have wished. Their scoop was historic and complete. All that marred his triumph was some tiresome scepticism in England, a certain hostility that he himself did much to provoke, above all by his venomous attacks on Kirk. Horace Waller was appalled by his behaviour. He caught him out at their first meeting in a perfectly barefaced lie, which Stanley treated, on detection, with the coolest unconcern; and he wrote off quickly to Livingstone to warn him of what was happening and to reproach him, tenderly but firmly, for lending his name to Stanley's accusations without waiting for Kirk's reply. It is a powerful, moving protest, and it shows the nobility of Waller's mind.

Meanwhile, Livingstone sat quietly at Unyanyembe, inactive until his new porters could arrive. It was a long wait, punctuated by a little intermittent news from the outside world. On 3 July he was grieved to learn that Murchison was dead : "the best friend I ever had—true, warm, and abiding—he loved me more than I deserved". He spent his time largely in reading and in his eternal, brooding observation of the things and people round him, from the geological structure of Central Africa to the games played by the children. At last, after five months, the waiting came to an end, and on 25 August he was off again, with his new party, to the west.

His plan was to march again round the southern end of Tanganyika and Bangweolo, making for the copper-mines of Katanga. According to local information, the great "fountains" lay eight days' journey south from there. Having found them, he would turn to the exploration of the Lualaba, which he believed took its rise from these "fountains"; he would travel down the river far enough to prove whether or not it was the upper Nile; and he would then return home.

It looked a simple, limited programme. But it was far beyond his strength. Three weeks after starting he was sick again. On 19 September he records : "I am ill with bowels, having eaten nothing for eight days." On the 21st, "rest here, as the complaint does not yield to medicine or time". So it goes on, almost without remission. His men said afterwards that he had "few periods of even comparative health from this date". By January they were back in the "sponges" round Lake Bangweolo, battling on through continuous, pelting rain. At times he had to be carried through the floods on the shoulders of his men—a vivid engraving of the scene appears in the published *Last Journals*. The entries in his diary get shorter, as the effort of writing them plainly increases. And yet there is still the old close observation, the susceptibility to natural beauty. He pauses at one moment to note all the varieties of wild flower he has come upon in the country he is passing through. He can still find a striking phrase : "The fish-eagle lifts up his remarkable voice. It is pitched in a high falsetto key, very loud, and seems as if he were calling to some one in the other world." Nothing can destroy his compassionate understanding of Africans, even when they hinder his progress : "Islanders are always troublesome," he notes reasonably, "from a sense of security in their fastnesses." And through it all the old tenacity remains : "Nothing earthly will make me give up my work in despair. I encourage myself in the Lord my God, and go forward."

But he could not go forward much farther. He was

stuck in those terrible swamps, and not all his determination, or the devotion of his men, could get him out of them. He was suffering from constant hæmorrhages, again and again obliged to stop and rest because he was too weak to go on. "It is not all pleasure this exploration", he notes, with grotesque mildness, on 19 April, and then, after a few lines more : "No observations now, owing to great weakness; I can scarcely hold the pencil, and my stick is a burden."

He was soon beyond walking, and his men made a stretcher for him, on which he was carried from 22 to 29 April. Repeatedly he had to ask them to put him down, as he could not bear the pain of the gentle motion, however slowly they went. For four days he could make no entry in his journal. Then, on 27 April, he resumes: "Knocked up quite, and remain—recover—sent to buy milch goats. We are on the banks of the Molilamo."

He wrote no more. On 29 April they reached the village of a chief named Chitambo, where they found accommodation in empty huts, for the harvest was approaching and the people were away watching their crops. It was then apparent that Livingstone could not be moved, and they left him in his bed. Towards midnight on the next day he had a brief conversation with Susi. "Is this the Luapula?" he asked. Being told where they were, he repeated the question : "How many days is it to the Luapula?" "I think it is three days, master", Susi replied. A little later he sent for Susi again and asked him to boil some water. When he brought it, Livingstone said: "All right, you can go out now." Those were his last words. About four o'clock the next morning (1 May) they found him kneeling by his bedside, his head buried in his hands. He was dead.

Livingstone's African followers now faced a formidable problem. They had lost their leader, whose orders they had been accustomed to accept without question, however incomprehensible they might be. They were in a strange country, hundreds of miles from home. Moreover, they felt themselves responsible for Livingstone's possessions, and for his body. There seems to have been no hesitation on the part of the men in deciding that they must all return to the coast, taking the corpse with them, and that Susi and Chuma must direct their march.

It was a most remarkable decision, clearly entailing endless difficulties and dangers : the final proof, if that was needed, of the reverence Livingstone inspired in his followers. Their first problem confronted them before ever they started. If Chitambo learnt of the white man's death, he might be expected to inflict a heavy fine upon the party, in compensation for the ill luck it would entail upon his people; and that would straiten their means so much that they would be too poor to reach the coast. Accordingly, they tried to keep the news secret. It was, of course, a hopeless attempt, and before the day was out Chitambo knew what had happened. He acted with unlooked-for generosity. He had travelled himself in earlier days, and he recognised that this death was an accident, for which no one was to blame. He advised them to bury the body straight away and give up their plan of carrying it to the coast; but when he found that they were determined to attempt the task, he desisted and gave them all the help he could.

The body was eviscerated and the heart buried on the spot. After a fortnight's exposure to the sun, during which time it was watched uninterruptedly by the men day and night, it was wrapped in the bark of a tree and a piece of sailcloth and then lashed to a pole, so that it could be carried by two men.

They did not attempt to follow exactly the route by which they had come. Instead, they went first northwestward, to cross the Luapula, and then north-east through the heart of the Bangweolo swamps, rejoining their earlier route to the north of the lake. Similarly, they avoided following the shore of Lake Tanganyika, as Livingstone had done, but took a more easterly, and a shorter, route to Unyanyembe. The journey was by no means easy, and at Chawende's, on the northern fringe of Lake Bangweolo, they had to fight. They came off victorious, and were allowed to proceed unmolested. Presently they were heartened by the news that a party of Englishmen was on its way from Bagamoyo. Chuma went forward to meet them, and on 20 October he found them at Unyanyembe. The party was a third "relief expedition", in the charge of Lieutenant Verney Lovett Cameron. When Livingstone's body arrived, Cameron did his best to persuade the bearers to bury it at Unyanyembe, partly because the country towards the coast was much disturbed and there would be the gravest risk in attempting to carry it on to Bagamoyo, and partly from a feeling that in any case Livingstone would have preferred to lie in an African grave, like his wife. But the men were adamant in believing it was their duty to see their master's body conveyed home, in spite of all difficulties, and Cameron gave way.

It was agreed that two Englishmen from the expedition should accompany them to the coast. They had not gone far before it became evident that if it was known they were carrying a corpse they would be stopped; and accordingly, pretending to send it back to Unyanyembe for burial, they repacked it in the disguise of a bale of trade goods. They had no further trouble on this score for the remainder of their journey. They reached Bagamoyo and handed over their charge to the acting British Consul, who arranged for the body to be taken to Zanzibar in a British warship. "And then", Waller cannot refrain from adding in his edition of the *Last Journals,* "it became perhaps rather too painfully plain to the men that their task was finished. . . . No sooner did they arrive at their journey's end than they were so far frowned out of notice that not so much as a passage to the Island was offered them when their burden was borne away."

Waller's protest was fully justified. Too little was said at the time of the work that these Africans did for Livingstone, and too little has been said on the matter since. They had been much more to him than an ordinary set of bearers. During the whole of the last stage of his journey, from Unyanyembe to Chitambo's, he had nothing but good to record of them—and we know from earlier experience that he did not fail to note the faults and crimes of his African companions. The conditions of that journey, in the pitiless rain through the Bangweolo swamps, were as bad as any that Livingstone ever called upon Africans to face; and though he led and directed the party through it all, for much of the time he was a physical burden to them. None of them understood, more than dimly, why he was travelling : most can have had not the smallest idea. Yet they served him with devotion till he died, and after his death they took the most difficult course open to them, in demonstration of their love and duty to him. They performed it to the full, with courage and unfailing resource.

The party owed most to its leaders, Chuma and Susi and the Nassick boy Jacob Wainwright, who alone of them all was literate. Yet even they scarcely received the recognition they had earned. Directly they arrived at the coast, as we have seen, Livingstone's body was taken out of their charge. Their services were at an end : they were abruptly dismissed. Later on, some small amends were made. Wainwright was brought over, at the expense of the Church Missionary Society, to attend Livingstone's funeral. Chuma and Susi, too, went to England and spent four months in Waller's rectory, at Twywell near Kettering, to help him with the work of editing their master's journals. He, at any rate, knew what Livingstone had owed them, and he did his best to see that their work was appreciated at its true value. But very few others understood the case as he did. Some of the sillier missionaries sentimentalised over them : most people simply ignored them, taking their achievement for granted. Yet Livingstone's countrymen owed them a great debt. They enabled him to spend his last painful months in the steady pursuit of the task to which he had dedicated himself; they stood by him at his death; they saw to it that his body returned home; they scrupulously preserved every particle of his possessions—and if one of them had been careless, or a knave like Musa, our text of the *Last Journals* might have been incomplete. They did, in fact, everything that could be required of any men. It is to be hoped that they did not feel the ingratitude of the world too keenly.

Livingstone's body was taken from Zanzibar to Aden. There it was transferred to the P. & O. liner *Malwa*, arriving at Southampton on 15 April 1874. The body was formally identified—by means of the fracture in the arm made by the lion in Bechuanaland thirty years earlier—and on 18 April it was buried in Westminster Abbey. The pall-bearers included Stanley, Kirk, Waller, Webb, and Jacob Wainwright. Old Robert Moffat was in the vast congregation. They sang Doddridge's great hymn:

> *O God of Bethel! by whose hand*
> *Thy people still are fed,*
> *Who through this weary pilgrimage*
> *Hast all our fathers led.*

A huge black slab was placed on the tomb, in the very centre of the nave. The inscription includes some words Livingstone used about the slave trade in a letter written a year before his death: "All I can say in my solitude is, may Heaven's rich blessing come down on every one— American, English, Turk—who will help to heal this open sore of the world."

Chapter Nine

Livingstone and Africa

THERE is apt to be something ironical, something forced and insincere, in the national tribute paid to a great man at his death. But the congregation at Livingstone's funeral, and the crowds in the streets outside, showed a true instinct. Their tribute was perfectly genuine, and it was the right one. During his lifetime Livingstone had been famous, and a part at least of his achievement had received the recognition it deserved. He had been given the freedom of cities and honorary degrees, and ovations from the great audiences he addressed. He had been received by the Queen. But all this was what a great explorer might have expected. The crowds on that April day in London showed that they knew he was much more than an explorer: more than a missionary too—no English missionary has ever had a national funeral, though some may well have deserved it. He was recognised by his countrymen as some one unique : an explorer and a missionary, but also a geographer, a scientist, a humanitarian statesman. Perhaps it would be nearest the truth to say that, with a simple intuition, those crowds knew him for what he was : a great and good man.

At the time of his death, though he was as determined and, in the long run, as optimistic as ever, Livingstone must have felt that he had failed. The Arab slave trade in East Africa continued, with all its horrors, the sickening miseries it involved for the Africans brought into contact with it. The geographical question he was struggling with remained unanswered. If only he could have known it, the decisive steps in the ending of the East African slave trade were to be taken, and the Nile-Lualaba-Congo problem solved, within five years of his death. And both those triumphs were directly due to him.

The attack on the East African slave trade had continued steadily while he was on his last journey. Since 1845 it had been based on a policy of restriction, successive Sultans of Zanzibar agreeing with the British government to limit the scope of the slavers, without declaring the whole trade unlawful. The Sultans' difficulties have to be remembered : to proclaim an outright abolition would have meant a social change so great as to endanger the stability of their regime. They were in an embarrassing situation, between their subjects, to whom slavery and the slave trade were part of the natural order and a powerful vested interest, and the British government, with which they were always anxious to stand well. In 1864 Sultan Majid was persuaded to issue a decree forbidding all transport of slaves during the period of the south-west monsoon (i.e. from January to April inclusive). This was an important step forward : for the "Northern Arabs", importing slaves from East Africa into Arabia and the Middle East, could not move their cargoes conveniently in their sailing dhows except during that period. Under the existing arrangements with the British government, that meant that any slaving ships caught by cruisers of the British slave squadron during these months would be condemned and their cargoes freed. Four years later this legislation was stiffened : any of the Sultan's East African subjects who co-operated with the "Northern Arabs" in slaving was to be liable to fine and imprisonment; and the Sultan wrote to the rulers on the Arabian coast warning them that "in future every northern dhow reaching Zanzibar shall be burned forthwith, as their sole business here is to steal the children of the inhabitants of Zanzibar and their slaves".

The law, then, was strong and explicit. But it was very imperfectly enforced, partly from the timidity and smallness of the Sultan's forces, and partly because the British government itself reduced its slave squadron on the coast in 1867–1868 as a measure of economy. For all the effort that was being made, it was estimated that 12,000 slaves were still being exported every year from Zanzibar and less than 900 intercepted and freed. On Sultan Majid's death in 1870 the British government tried to conclude a new, more effective agreement with his successor, Barghash, but Barghash rejected the proposals put before him and the negotiations broke down.

The policy of restriction was clearly a failure, and the British government now turned to consider whether or not it should impose a policy of abolition. The first step was to appoint a Parliamentary Committee to investigate the whole subject. It examined fourteen witnesses in July 1871 and produced a report, recommending that the government should take measures to secure the entire abolition of the East African slave trade. The Committee understood well enough that this would mean hard bargaining with the new Sultan of Zanzibar, who had already turned down much less drastic proposals, but they were sure that no compromise was possible, that "any attempt to supply slaves for domestic use in Zanzibar will always be a pretext and cloak for a foreign trade".

The government accepted these arguments and put them into effect. A special diplomatic mission was appointed in 1872, under Sir Bartle Frere, to go out to Zanzibar and negotiate a treaty on the lines the Committee had suggested. Frere's assignment was a difficult one. Sultan Barghash was stiffly opposed to the idea of abolition, and much inclined to seek support and help from other powers, notably France and the United States, against what could easily be represented as a piece of British bullying. The diplomatic discussions took a month, and at the end of that time the Sultan flatly refused to conclude the treaty. There was nothing for Frere to do but to leave.

On learning the news of Frere's failure, the British government decided that much stronger pressure was required. At the beginning of June, Kirk (who was now Consul at Zanzibar) was ordered to inform the Sultan that if he did not consent at once to the terms of the Frere treaty, the island would be blockaded by a British naval force. Two days' argument followed, and then the Sultan gave way. On 5 June the treaty was signed.

It came into force at once. The great Zanzibar slave-market was shut down the same day. Naturally, the treaty did not achieve complete success. Slaves continued to be smuggled along the coast, though in diminishing numbers. An important hindrance to total abolition remained, in that it was still permissible to transport slaves through the Sultan's dominions by land. But that was forbidden by a further agreement in 1876. Thereafter, the Arab slave trade in East Africa was virtually at an end, lingering on furtively on a very small scale, but as an organised trade quite dead. Finally, after Zanzibar had become a British protectorate, the institution of slavery itself was abolished in 1897.

Livingstone died just five weeks before the crucial treaty of 1873 was signed. It was hard that he should not have known of it; for it was to him, more than to any other man, that its conclusion was really due. The British government had indeed embarked on its policy of restriction before Livingstone knew anything of East Africa. He started to learn about the Arab slave trade when he was in the Makololo country in 1853, but he did not come into close contact with it until six years later, at the time of his discovery of Lake Nyasa. It then began to take a prominent place in his mind, side by side with the Portuguese slave trade. The experience of the Zambesi Expedition encouraged him to believe that the suppression of the Portuguese trade could be achieved by means of naval action and diplomatic pressure on the Portuguese government: at all events, that there was nothing more he could do, in the existing conditions, to help it forward. Instead, he turned his whole attention to the Arab slave trade, and in the last nine years of his life—first of all at home and

then in Africa—he did everything he could to press on
the attack on it, through his published writings, by
correspondence, by the ceaseless noting of information
that might ultimately be used as evidence. He can fairly
be said to have led public opinion in this matter. The
missionary societies listened to him : that might be taken
almost for granted. But so did British governments:
Clarendon continued to support him as firmly as old
Palmerston had done. His dispatches home were published and discussed eagerly, in Parliament, in *The Times,*
at the Royal Geographical Society. After his meeting with
Stanley his ideas gained a wider circulation still through
the *New York Herald.*

It would be wrong and absurd to suggest that Livingstone alone was responsible for the ending of the East
African slave trade. Much of the credit belongs to the
British Foreign Office and to successive British representa-
tives at Zanzibar, above all, Kirk. If it was sad that
Livingstone should have died just too soon to know of
the successful completion of the task, it was even sadder
that he should have been ignorant of Kirk's staunch
and persistent part in getting the treaty signed. Yet when
all proper recognition has been given to the men responsible on the spot and in London, it was Livingstone who
led them, who gave point to their work and secured them
a sufficient backing from governments and public opinion
to enable them to achieve success.

The other great problem that occupied Livingstone's
mind on his last journey was geographical. From the bare
records of the closing weeks of his life, it seems that this
problem had come to dominate his mind. The very last
words he wrote were concerned with the name of a river.
"How many days is it to the Luapula?" was the last
question he asked. His death left a vital problem unsolved. It turned first on the Lualaba. What was this
mysterious great river, flowing to the north? Was it the
Nile, as Livingstone firmly believed? Or was it the Congo,

only the lower reaches of which were as yet marked on the maps?

A part of the answer was suggested very quickly, by V. L. Cameron, the leader of the last "Livingstone relief expedition". He had arranged for Livingstone's body to be dispatched to the coast from Unyanyembe, but he did not go down with it himself. His instructions had been to assist Livingstone and put himself under his direction, in order to supplement his work. He thought it his duty to pursue that supplementation even though Livingstone was dead. Accordingly, he now set out westwards, to examine the country beyond Lake Tanganyika. In the course of his journey he travelled some way up the basin of the Lualaba, and he came to hold the strong opinion that it was associated with the Congo, not the Nile. He did not settle the question, since he pressed on southward, made his way over the highlands to Lake Dilolo (which Livingstone had passed on his journey of 1852–1856), and thence to Benguela on the west coast.

Meanwhile, another traveller, more directly under Livingstone's influence, had begun to try to solve the Lualaba problem. After he had reported the "finding" of Livingstone in England, Stanley returned to America. He then served as correspondent of the *New York Herald* with the British forces in the Ashanti War of 1873–1874. On his way back, at St. Vincent in the West Indies, he learnt of Livingstone's death. At once he began to consider the possibility of taking up and completing Livingstone's work. He set off for London, arriving in time to act as a pall-bearer at the funeral. Not long afterwards he asked the *Daily Telegraph* if it would be interested in sending him out to Central Africa again, to try to solve the most pressing of its geographical problems—the structure of Lake Albert and its relation to Victoria Nyanza, the outflow of Lake Tanganyika, the identity of the Lualaba, the upper course of the Congo. The *Daily Telegraph* agreed to finance the expedition jointly with the *New York Herald*, and Stanley set out in the autumn. In the course of a huge journey lasting three years (1874–1877)—probably the longest journey ever undertaken in Africa by a single explorer—he threw light on all the questions he had set out to answer. He found that Victoria Nyanza was indeed one enormous lake, as Speke had claimed, and not a group of lakes. He demonstrated that Tanganyika had no outlet. And making his way across to Nyangwe, whence Livingstone had turned back in loathing after the massacre of 1871, he followed the course of the Lualaba, round the vast arc that it makes through the very centre of Africa, and out to the Atlantic at Boma. He had proved that Livingstone's tenacious supposition was, after all, mistaken : the Lualaba was in fact the upper Congo.

Stanley's journey of 1874–1877 was a very different affair from any of Livingstone's. His equipment was lavish, including a train that, at the outset, comprised 356 porters. He marched with the utmost speed, where it had always been Livingstone's habit to move no faster than was convenient, stopping to ask questions and learn about the country as he went, and to put up with delays. Stanley made no attempt to pretend that his expedition was conducted on Livingstone's peaceful principles. "My methods will not be Livingstone's", he wrote in his diary before he went out. "Each man has his own way. His, I think, had its defects, though the old man, personally, has been almost Christ-like for goodness, patience, and self-sacrifice. The selfish and wooden-headed world requires mastering, as well as loving charity." The Africans whom Stanley encountered soon found out what he meant by "mastering": it involved a ruthless brutality, above all an impatience, that was alien to Livingstone and to everything he believed in.[1]

The consequences of this great expedition were im-

---

[1] *The Autobiography of Sir Henry Morton Stanley* (1909), 295. For some examples of Stanley's conduct on the journey and of contemporary comment on it, see Sir R. Coupland, *The Exploitation of East Africa* (1939), 325–9.

mediate and momentous. In 1876, while Stanley was on the later stages of his journey, an "International African Association" was founded in Brussels, under the direct patronage of King Leopold II of the Belgians. In form, it was a body of scientists, concerned with geographical and other similar problems. In practice, however, its objects were political. It immediately began to concern itself with the economic development of Central Africa. At first its attention was given to the East African interior, and it established a base at Karema, on the eastern shore of Lake Tanganyika. But Stanley had revealed the great potentialities of the Congo basin, and as soon as he returned home King Leopold tried to secure his services. There was some delay: Stanley was anxious to interest the British government in the region, and it was only when this attempt had failed that he accepted the terms Leopold offered him. He went out to the Congo in January 1879 and spent five and a half years there, laying the foundation of what came to be known as the Congo Free State, nominally independent, but in fact under Leopold's control and closely linked with the Belgian kingdom.

The carving out of the Congo Free State, sandwiched between the older colonial territories of France and Portugal, was the first chapter in the Scramble for Africa. In the course of the next ten years (1885–1895) the whole of Tropical Africa, with slight exceptions, passed under the control of European powers. Suddenly the political map took on very much the appearance it wears today. France possessed herself of the whole of north-western Africa except the four British territories, the two annexed by Germany, and the minor colonies of Spain and Portugal. In East Africa, Britain was the principal gainer, dividing with Germany the country between the great lakes and the sea. Since then the Congo Free State has been converted into a Belgian colony; the German territories have passed to Britain, France, and Belgium, under the mandate system after the First World War: but otherwise, apart from minor changes of boundary, the partition effected in the eighties and nineties has endured.

Coming as it did, the Scramble was what its name implies: a haphazard business of smash-and-grab, conducted with no rules except those of diplomacy, and without attention to the wishes or interests of Africans. Yet in some ways it offered a great opportunity—an opportunity to put into effect some of the principles that Livingstone, among others, had constantly preached. Tropical Africa could now be opened up to civilisation, with railways and roads, with European knowledge of hygiene and medicine and dietetics, with an intelligent, soundly based system of education. All this was possible. How quickly and how effectively would it be brought about?

It is tempting to think what Livingstone would have made of the Scramble for Africa. After all, he was only sixty when he died: he might easily have lived to see it. There is no doubt that he would have entirely disapproved of the way in which it was effected. But he would probably have recognised that it was a logical consequence of his work. This is most obvious on the Congo, where Stanley was taking over, completing, and greatly extending the task he had himself begun. But it is true also, and in a stricter sense, farther south, in the country round Lake Nyasa, which Livingstone himself discovered. There, too, his death led directly to two enterprises that were ultimately of political significance.

A month after the funeral in Westminster Abbey, a scheme was put before the United Free Church of Scotland for the establishment of a mission in Central Africa to commemorate Livingstone's work. The idea originated with James Stewart, who was now Principal of the important missionary institution at Lovedale in Cape Colony. Stewart had been disappointed and shocked by what he saw of the Zambesi Expedition, but in the plan he now proposed he set out to further the kind of work that Livingstone had had most at heart. The mission he envisaged was to be "of an industrial as well as an educational nature"; and it was to be founded on Lake Nyasa by men of Livingstone's own communion and country. The plan was well received, £10,000 was quickly forthcoming to assist it, and in 1875 the first party arrived on the lake, equipped with a small steamship such as Livingstone had laboured so energetically to establish there fifteen years earlier. An institution was set up, called Livingstonia, after the model of Lovedale, comprising in the end mission, school, industrial settlement, and hospital in one. Its presiding spirit was Robert Laws, who directed its work for fifty years, until he retired in 1927.

Not to be outdone by the Free Church, the Established Church of Scotland also sent out a mission, in 1876, to work in the country Livingstone had discovered. It was set not on the lake but in the Shire Highlands; and its centre was named after his birthplace, Blantyre.

Both these missions were handicapped by the difficulties of communication with the world outside. An effort was made to build a road from the east coast to Lake Nyasa, but it was unsuccessful. The alternative was Livingstone's route, by water, up the Zambesi through Portuguese territory and into the Shire. The missions were not well fitted to maintain a service of this kind, and it was decided in 1878 to set up an "African Lakes Company", partly to perform this function and partly to develop the ivory trade, using free labour, in competition with the Arab traders, who still employed slaves. This was exactly the policy Livingstone had urged during the Zambesi Expedition. It was less successful than the founders of the company had hoped it would be, for it was handicapped by insufficient capital, by mismanagement, and by constant trouble with its Arab competitors. It never grew into a powerful corporation, like the British South Africa Company in Rhodesia, a little farther to the south. But, with the missions, it established British influence in the Shire valley and on the western side of Lake Nyasa, which led in 1889–1891 to the proclamation of a formal British protectorate.

British control meant not only the destruction of the lingering slave trade on Lake Nyasa, a settled law and order where war had been raging ever since Livingstone's first visits to the country. It entailed important economic changes also—notably the establishment of tobacco-planting as a new and soon flourishing industry, under European supervision and control. For Livingstone's prophecy of the future of the Shire Highlands has been largely fulfilled. The settlement of white men began there in the 1890s; a railway linking Blantyre with the Shire was completed in 1908; 4,000 Europeans now live in the country, not merely as administrators or visiting traders but as its permanent citizens.

Though Livingstone never showed himself interested in political annexation and hoisted no flags in Africa, it was directly owing to his work, and to the inspiration he left behind him, that this territory passed under British control—an important element in the new Central African federation that was formed in 1953. In the simple words of an official report, "Nyasaland is Livingstone's country".[1]

Livingstone's work, then, led, clearly and directly, to three great consequences : the abolition of the Arab slave trade; the solution of the chief problem of Central African geography; the development of British enterprise —missionary, economic, in the end political—in the country round Lake Nyasa, as a part of the Scramble for Africa as a whole, to which he also contributed. But the significance of his work does not stop there. Behind all this, and transcending it, lies a greater achievement still: the change he helped to effect in the thinking of Europeans about Africans.

Something has been said already, in Chapter Two, of the estimation in which Africans were held in Europe when Livingstone's career began. He had not been long in Africa before he realised that it was mistaken. In the writing of the *Missionary Travels* and in the speeches he

[1] *Colonial Reports: Nyasaland, 1952* (1954), 125.

made at home, he was at pains to emphasise that the
ordinary Englishman's idea of the African was a caricature. "Englishmen are very apt to form their opinion of
Africans", he observed in the Senate House at Cambridge, "from the elegant figures in tobacconists' shops;
I scarcely think such are fair specimens." Moreover, since
a high proportion of the Africans seen by Europeans
were slaves or the descendants of slaves, he thought it just
to point out, in his speech at Bath in 1864, that it was
usually criminals who were sold into slavery: "The
crimes may not always be very great, but I conjecture,
from the extreme ugliness of many slaves, that they were
the degraded criminal classes; and it is not fair to take
the typical negro from among them, any more than it
would be to place 'Bill Sykes' or some of *Punch*'s
garrotters as the typical John Bull."

Livingstone tried from the outset to see Africans as they
really were, with sympathy but without sentimentality.
We can scarcely realise now how difficult a feat that was.
It demanded a questing intelligence, openness of judgment, and candour in acknowledging mistakes. All these
faculties he had; and they were informed by the truest
Christian compassion, which enabled him to understand
what other people only laughed at or condemned.

The simple proposition from which he started was that
Africans were in no sense a separate species from Europeans: that they were fundamentally the same. This was
not a new idea. At the outset of the Revolution the
French Assembly was invited "to consecrate the principle
of philanthropy which makes of the human race one
family". In abolitionist propaganda in England the kneeling slave had asked: "Am I not a man and a brother?"
But Livingstone had no interest in the theoretical rights
of man, and he saw through the rhetoric of that insufficient question. Other people did, too, and it led
them to turn away in revulsion from the whole humanitarian movement, as far as it concerned Africans, to urge
that there was much more important work to be done

with the English poor, that that must come first. "The work at home must be completed thoroughly," wrote Dickens in 1848, "or there is no hope abroad. To your tents, O Israel! but see they are your own tents! Set *them* in order; leave nothing to be done *there*; and outpost will convey your lesson on to outpost until the naked armies of King Obi and King Boy are reached, and taught." [1]

Livingstone never made the mistake of forgetting the miseries of his own poor countrymen in favour of a sentimental fuss over Africans. He sprang from the working class himself; and Glasgow could show then—as it can still—a wretchedness and suffering as dismal as any in Britain. In a speech of 1857 he remarked: "I do not think better of the Africans for being black, because if I were not a missionary to them, I believe I should be a missionary to the poor in London." But his intuition was perfectly right. His peculiar gift lay in understanding the African and explaining him, and his needs, to Europe.

From this first position everything else followed. Livingstone believed passionately in the value of Christianity to the Africans. But while preaching his religion to them, he made it his business to try to understand their religion too, their social customs, and the reasons that lay at the root of them. Early in his career in Bechuanaland, he began to learn something of the initiation rites known as the *Boguera*; and at once, instinctively, he doubted the wisdom of the older missionaries in condemning them. He would not go beyond noting his doubt. But in 1857 he printed it, and the next year he directed the particular attention of his brother-in-law, at the outset of his work as a missionary, to this matter: "Is there anything really irreligious in the Boguera? Or is it anything more than a political rite?"

It was the same in the whole field of African religion. He wanted first to *know*, not to judge or condemn. In Chapter XXV of the *Narrative* of the Zambesi Expedi-

[1] "The Niger Expedition," *Household Words*, 19 August 1848. Reprinted in *Miscellaneous Papers* (1914), 123.

tion, he summarised his knowledge of the subject. Like any man of his age and calling, he was bound to set it out in moral terms: yet, allowing for that, what he has to say is hardly different in spirit from the verdict of a modern anthropologist. He looks at human sacrifice, at cannibalism, at witchcraft, at fetish, and he is not shocked by any of them. He emphasises, moreover, that the first two practices have been found only in a few places—correcting, once again, the impression of his countrymen that they were universal in Africa.

This does not imply that Livingstone expressed any approval of practices like these. His serene conviction of the paramount values of Christianity was never shaken for a moment in the smallest degree. It gave the meaning to all his work, making it not merely analytical but constructive. This, again, he shared with many other Christians of his time. He differed from them, and went beyond them, in this : that he never patronised Africans or showed, from his words or behaviour, that he thought himself superior to them. A simple illustration of this comes from old Adam Sedgwick, one of the most distinguished of Livingstone's admirers. In a letter written in 1858, prefacing the published text of the Cambridge lectures, he argued earnestly that Englishmen had as many follies and crimes to be ashamed of as Africans, "that the poor African is of a moral nature in the exact similitude of our own . . . that he is indeed our humble Brother". Livingstone would have subscribed to all that, except for the one word "humble". This is what betrays Sedgwick's attitude, showing that he had not really grasped Livingstone's teaching in its full implications. To Livingstone all men were alike in nature : where they differed was in capacity and opportunity.

Looking back over nearly a century, we can see how original this conception was, how fertile it has subsequently been. Livingstone's contemporaries understood it very dimly. Sedgwick's words represented a liberal, not a reactionary, point of view. The old inherent assumption that Europe's moral superiority over Africa was as great as her technical ascendancy remained—entrenched, indeed, as we have seen, by the missionaries themselves.

There were, moreover, a few people who reacted as violently against Livingstone's teaching as Dickens had reacted against the earlier humanitarians. They distrusted his sympathetic interpretation of Africans : instead, they emphasised their barbarism and denied their capability of self-improvement. These critics found a spokesman in Richard Burton, who devoted a strident and challenging chapter in his *Mission to Gelele, King of Dahome* (1864), to "the Negro's Place in Nature". "The negro, in mass," he wrote, "will not improve beyond a certain point, and that not respectable; he mentally remains a child, and is never capable of a generalisation. ... He is nought but self; he lacks even the rude virtue of hospitality. . . . The removal of the negro from Africa is like sending a boy to school; it is his only chance of improvement, of learning that there is something more in life than drumming and dancing, talking and singing, drinking and killing."

These views must not be taken too seriously. Burton was, as usual, out to shock; and like a good many Englishmen, then and since, whose work had lain first in Asia, he formed a natural antipathy towards Africa when he arrived there. As an aggressive free-thinker and a man who liked best to be in a minority of one, he did not pretend to admire Livingstone. No doubt, too, there was something of jealousy in his attitude, for, with all his talents, he never came near achieving Livingstone's popularity and fame. Yet there is something significant in these words, for all their crudity and spite. Burton takes pride to himself, in this very chapter, for his support of the new science of anthropology, which was just beginning to emerge, largely as a result of the Darwinian controversy. Whatever the grounds for his views or the motives that lay behind this expression of them, they do represent a fresh effort to get away from the vague and stultifying sentimentality that had hitherto dominated the thinking of Englishmen about Africans. But Livingstone has been victorious in the end. Allowing for the differences between the intellectual background of that age and this, the modern anthropologist has much more to learn about Africans from him than from Burton.

It has often been observed that Livingstone's relations with his European companions showed little of the sure instinct and sympathy he always extended to Africans. No difference of principle was involved : Europeans and Africans were, to him, simply men. But he expected from Europeans a combination of qualities and powers like his own. Fear, stupidity, sickness, he swept them all aside as unworthy weaknesses, as contemptible as laziness or dishonesty. It is heroic and inspiring, for he drove himself harder than any one else; but it revealed a deep psychological miscalculation, which he never made in dealing with Africans. He understood their capabilities and he did not require of them more than they could reasonably be asked to perform. The exceptions to that rule are rare. The most striking of them—the examination of the Kebrabasa Rapids in 1858—is recorded with candour by Livingstone himself : as he drove the Makololo forward over the scorching rocks, they told Kirk that they thought he had gone mad. He had no comparable conception of what could be expected of Europeans—or even of himself : the tasks he undertook on his second and third journeys all proved beyond his powers to complete.

In his dealings with Europeans, moreover, there was a curious infirmity of judgment that he never displayed with Africans. "I have rarely, if ever, seen a man so easily led as Dr. Livingstone", noted one observer.[1] The whole history of his relations with his colleagues on the Zambesi Expedition is a commentary on that remark. There can be no doubt whatever that his brother's mischief-making lay at the bottom of all those troubles. Livingstone did in the end admit that Charles's appoint-

[1] W. C. Devereux, *A Cruise in the "Gorgon"* (1869), 233.

ment had been a great mistake. Yet he was so little self-aware that in writing to Waller in 1871 he could refer to the story that Charles had led him into injustice towards Baines and add : "I am just the weakling to be so led." [1] He was not, of course, a weakling; but he did not feel at home in close association with Europeans, and he never knew quite where he stood with them. He tried to exact far too much of them; and when the fulfilment of his dearest plans depended upon them, wholly or in part, the least of their shortcomings became a crime. This being so, it is not surprising that all the white men associated with him on the Zambesi Expedition came to dislike him, to regard him, at the least, as impossible to work with. But it must be added that the finer spirits among them, for all their temporary disillusionment, returned to a permanent admiration for him afterwards: not only Kirk (who wrote some extremely bitter things about him at the close of the Expedition), but Waller and James Stewart also. [2]

The same principle lies at the back of his attitude towards missionaries. Because he thought their work so important, he judged them by a higher standard than other men. His anger at their faults and failures was correspondingly sharpened. This is true throughout his career, from his very first months in Africa to the end of his life. To him, the proper function of a missionary there was to work with people hitherto beyond the reach of Christianity. The multiplication of missionaries, close to one another, in Cape Colony shocked him. Timid new men, he wrote sarcastically in 1853, "will discover some important and very large field of labour a long way south of the Orange river in which they will be associated with a Wesleyan, a Church of England clergyman, a Dutch Predicant, and a government schoolmaster, each

[1] Livingstone to Waller, November 1871 : Waller Papers (Rhodes House, Oxford).

[2] See the very important *Zambesi Journal of James Stewart*, ed. J. P. R. Wallis (1952), especially pp. xiv, xxi, 260–5.

of whom considers the ten shanties and eight shop-keepers' houses as his 'sphere of labour' involving the most excrutiating responsibility". As for missionary politics at home, they filled him with contempt. "You may think now that the missionary field is a queer one", he remarked to his brother-in-law. "Queer things are said and sung in it; but never mind, my friend."

What angered him more than anything was sectarian squabbles, in the face of all the vast work that had still to be done. We return again here to Livingstone's magnanimity. For one who grew up amid the doctrinal and political quarrels that led to the disruption of the Church of Scotland in 1843, Livingstone's freedom from sectarian prejudice is extraordinary. He remained a Scottish Presbyterian all his life. But we have seen that, as a matter of organisation, he favoured a Church of England mission to the Zambesi. When he stayed with the Webbs at Newstead, he attended Anglican worship in the chapel of the house, communicating once a month. On his journeys he read the services of the Book of Common Prayer. Some people, whose piety was of a more formal kind than his, were outraged to note that, on the Zambesi Expedition, Sunday was not always observed as a day of rest. One critic thought that this was a sign that "Dr. Livingstone's feelings have undergone a change, and his fame as a traveller has eclipsed that as a missionary". The inference was not correct. On the last journey Livingstone normally rested on Sundays; but it was characteristic of him that he was not a rigid Sabbatarian —if there was work that must be done to further the great overriding purposes of his travelling, it must be done on Sundays as well as on weekdays.

Most remarkable of all, Livingstone found much that was good to say of "our Roman Catholic fellow-Christians"—a surprising phrase in itself, coming from a mid-Victorian Scot. He always spoke of the early Jesuit missionaries in Angola with great respect : "these devoted men are still held in high estimation throughout the country to this day," he noted in 1854. "All speak well of them." He paid a generous tribute, too, to the work of the Roman Catholic Bishop of Angola, which he saw for himself at Loanda. Here again Livingstone appears great enough to stand outside the beliefs and ideas in which he had been brought up, to note everything, from wherever it might come, that contributed to the benefit of Africa and its people.

That was the sole end he had at heart. Some people were repelled by his monomania. One casual acquaintance noted that he talked well about Africa, but not about anything else. Many critics thought he treated his wife badly, subordinating her health, and the interests of his whole family, to his own work: as old Trader Horn put it in his growling way, "dragging that poor girl, Mary Moffat, along until she was forced to a long rest in her grave".[1] There is no evidence at all that his wife saw it in that light : her only desire was to be at his side whenever she could do anything to help him. And it is plain enough that he himself felt keenly his long separations from his family. On the last journey he repeatedly displays a yearning to finish his work and go home. But work came before everything, and that, for him, lay in Africa, not in Europe. In his heart he must always have known that he would die there. As he put it once, with a perfect simplicity : "We seem immortal till our work is done."

These criticisms are, in fact, out of scale. They might be appropriate in dealing with an ordinary man. But Livingstone was ordinary in nothing. The tasks he set himself were stupendous, and he knew he must assault them in his own way. It did not always prove to be the right way. He had to learn by experience, for example, that he could not manage white men, and he learnt it by mismanaging them, causing them to suffer and suffering himself. Such lessons did not come easily to him. He was rigid, stubborn, unreasonable, too quickly prone to

[1] *Trader Horn* (Florin Books ed.), 148.

contempt. These faults were always there, but for most of his life they were kept out of sight because he was dealing with Africans. With them he had an overriding patience and charity, an exact sense of what they were able to do.

Other travellers have marched as many miles as Livingstone: a few have made discoveries of even greater geographical importance. But the span of his whole achievement is something unique. In addition to his geographical work, he made valuable contributions to linguistics, to tropical medicine, to ethnology, and the study of comparative religion. In the field of public policy, he directed the final attack on the East African slave trade, and he pointed the way to the constructive development of the country, by Europeans and Africans in co-operation. By his practice just as much as by his words, he showed Africans the help and comfort that the teachings of Christ had to offer them. His simple, direct, unpatronising love for them was the foundation on which his whole work was built. It informed and inspired what was perhaps the greatest of all his achievements: the interpretation of the African to the European.

In 1913 the Royal Geographical Society held a special meeting to commemorate the centenary of Livingstone's birth. The opening speech was made by the Society's President, Lord Curzon. Nobody could have been more widely different from Livingstone. Yet on that occasion Curzon summed up his work in a few noble sentences that have not been bettered by any one :

"In the course of his wonderful career, Livingstone served three masters. As a missionary he was the sincere and zealous servant of God. As an explorer he was the indefatigable servant of science. As a denouncer of the slave trade he was the fiery servant of humanity. . . . His spirit hovers over Central Africa, just as that of Cecil Rhodes, of many of whose ideals he was the unconscious parent, broods over the South African regions that bear his name. And, though Africa has changed since Livingstone's day beyond all human recognition; though settled territories and demarcated frontiers have taken the place of lawlessness and intertribal warfare; though geographical problems which he went down to the grave without having solved are now among the commonplaces of school primers; though exploration has given way to peaceful evolution, and railways have replaced the tortuous crawl of the caravan; though Africa is not merely a European interest, but has almost become a European possession—yet the work of Livingstone still stands forth in monumental grandeur among the achievements of human energy, and the spirit of Livingstone will continue to inspire a generation that knew him not, but will never cease to revere his name." [1]

[1] *Geographical Journal* (1913), xli. 422–3.

Note on Sources

1. PUBLISHED WORKS

Missionary Travels and Researches in South Africa (1857); *Narrative of an Expedition to the Zambesi and its Tributaries* (1865); *The Last Journals of David Livingstone in Central Africa* (2 vols., 1874). A selection from these books appears in *Livingstone's Travels*, ed. J. I. Macnair, with geographical sections by R. Miller (1954).

2. LETTERS

No collected edition of Livingstone's letters has ever been made. Several hundreds have been preserved. They frequently repeat one another verbatim, and passages from them are sometimes transcribed into the published books. An interesting series, relating chiefly to the earlier period of Livingstone's life, appears in *Some Letters from Livingstone,* ed. D. Chamberlin (1940). Twenty-one more are printed in *The Matabele Mission*, ed. J. P. R. Wallis (1945) : they date from 1858 to 1864 and were all written to Livingstone's brother-in-law, John Smith Moffat. Among the collections of unpublished letters may be mentioned those written to Edmund Gabriel, British Consul at Loanda, in 1854–1855 (British Museum, Add. MS. 37410); those to Kirk, in the Kirk Papers, Rhodes House Library, Oxford; and the very important series of eighty-five (1862–1872) to Horace Waller, in the Waller Papers in the same library.

Letters and dispatches of an official nature are printed in the *Parliamentary Papers* and the *Proceedings of the Royal Geographical Society*. The originals of many of them are in the Public Record Office, mainly within the files F.O. 63 and 84. The planning of the Zambesi Expedition and negotiations with the government can be followed in detail in F.O. 63/842.

Any student of Livingstone's work must make use of the magnificent collection of material assembled in the Scottish National Memorial to David Livingstone at Blantyre. For an account of its formation, see J. I. Macnair, *The Story of the Scottish National Memorial to David Livingstone* (n.d.). The collection includes personal relics of all kinds, letters, and a number of Livingstone's original notebooks, a fresh study of which, in the light of modern geographical knowledge, may modify at some points the accepted accounts of Livingstone's travels. Cf. J. I. Macnair, "Some Recovered Relics of David Livingstone", *Geographical Journal,* cxviii (1952), 58–60; and F. Debenham, "New Light on Livingstone's Last Journey", *ibid.,* cxx (1954), 1–14.

3. BIOGRAPHIES

The official biography was written by W. G. Blaikie: *The Personal Life of David Livingstone* (1880 and many subsequent editions). It is based on a good deal of material in the possession of Livingstone's family, to which later biographers have not had access.

Among other biographies, the following are valuable: T. Hughes, *David Livingstone* (1889); H. H. Johnston, *Livingstone and the Exploration of Central Africa* (1891); A. Z. Fraser, *Livingstone and Newstead* (1913); R. J. Campbell, *Livingstone* (1929); J. I. Macnair, *Livingstone the Liberator* (1940); Sir R. Coupland, *Livingstone's Last Journey* (1945). See also *Dr. Livingstone's Cambridge Lectures,* ed. W. Monk (2nd ed., 1860).

4. OTHER WORKS

The following books written by, or about, people associated with Livingstone are of value for his life : V. L. Cameron, *Across Africa* (2 vols., 1877); Sir R. Coupland, *Kirk on the Zambesi* (1928); W. C. Devereux, *A Cruise in the "Gorgon"* (1869); J. S. Moffat, *The Lives of Robert and Mary Moffat* (2nd ed., 1886); W. E. Oswell, *William Cotton Oswell, Hunter and Explorer* (2 vols., 1900); H. M. Stanley, *How I Found Livingstone* (1872. For some important differences between the first two editions and their successors, see Coupland, *Livingstone's Last Journey*, 211–12); *The Autobiography of Sir Henry Morton Stanley, G.C.B.* (1909); *The Zambesi Journal of James Stewart*, ed. J. P. R. Wallis (1952); J. P. R. Wallis, *Thomas Baines of King's Lynn* (1941); E. D. Young, *The Search after Livingstone* (1868).

For the general historical background, see Sir R. Coupland, *The Exploitation of East Africa, 1856–1890* (1939); K. S. Latourette, *History of the Expansion of Christianity* (1939–1945), vol. v; R. Oliver, *The Missionary Factor in East Africa* (1952); R. Lovett, *History of the London Missionary Society* (2 vols., 1899); A. E. M. Anderson-Morshead, *History of the Universities Mission to Central Africa* (1909); G. H. Wilson, *History of the Universities Mission to Central Africa* (1936).

Index

177

INDEX

960   7078

960   7078
Simmons, J.
Livingstone and Africa

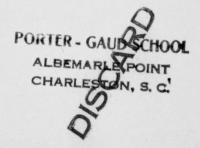

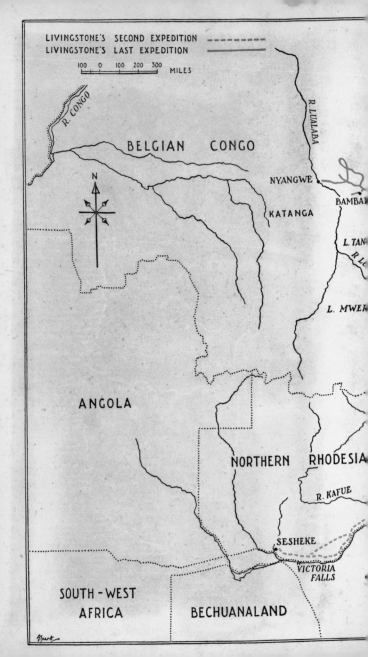